Steck-Vaughn Phonics

LEVEL D

Reviewers

Terese D'Amico
Gifted Education Specialist for Grades 3–6
Thomas Jefferson Magnet School
Euclid, Ohio

Dinah Costello
Third Grade Teacher/Assistant Principal
Holy Angels School
Colma, California

Sandy Harrison
First Grade Teacher/Instructional Coordinator
Joe Wright Elementary School
Jacksonville, Texas

Dr. Marti O'Brien
Resource Specialist for Alternative Education
Polk County Schools
Bartow, Florida

Terry Redd
Second Grade Teacher
Don Shute Elementary School
East Peoria, Illinois

ISBN 0-8172-8379-X

Copyright © 1999 Steck-Vaughn Company

Printed in the United States of America

6 7 8 9 10 11 12 WC 06 05 04 03

STECK-VAUGHN
ELEMENTARY · SECONDARY · ADULT · LIBRARY

A Harcourt Company

www.steck-vaughn.com

Level D Contents

Acknowledgments

Grateful acknowledgment is made to the following authors, agents, and publishers for permission to use copyrighted materials. Every effort has been made to trace ownership of all copyrighted material and to secure the necessary permissions to reprint. We express regret in advance for any error or omission. Any oversight will be acknowledged in future printings.

"Dictionary" from *Laughing Time: Collected Nonsense* by William Jay Smith. Copyright © 1990 by William Jay Smith. Reprinted by permission of Farrar, Straus & Giroux, Inc.

"Do Spiders Stick to Their Own Webs?" from *Where Fish Go in Winter and Other Great Mysteries* by Amy Goldman Koss. Copyright © 1987 by Amy Goldman Koss. Used by permission of Price Stern & Sloan, Inc., a division of Penguin Putnam, Inc.

"It Fell in the City" from *Blackberry Ink* (Morrow Jr. Books) by Eve Merriam. Copyright © 1985 by Eve Merriam. Reprinted by permission of Marian Reiner.

"June Is a Tune that Jumps on a Stair." Reprinted with the permission of Simon & Schuster Books for Young Readers, an imprint of Simon & Schuster Children's Publishing Division from *Song and Dance* by Sarah Wilson. Copyright © 1992 Sarah Wilson.

"Pachycephalosaurus" by Richard Armour from *Poems Children Will Sit Still For.* Copyright by the Estate of Richard Armour. Reprinted by permission of Kathleen S. Armour.

Pronunciation symbols from *The Lincoln Writing Dictionary* by Christopher Morris, copyright © 1989 by Harcourt Brace & Company and copyright © 1998 First Steck-Vaughn Edition. Reproduced by permission of Harcourt Brace & Company.

Cover Design Design Five, NYC
Cover Illustration Maryjane Begin
Cover Photo © Renee Lynn/Tony Stone Images
Executive Editor Stephanie Muller
Senior Supervising Editor Carolyn Hall
Associate Director of Design Cynthia Ellis
Senior Design Manager Pamela Heaney
Designer Jessica Bristow
Asset Manager Margie Foster
Electronic Production Specialist Alan Klemp
Editorial Development, Design, and Production
The Quarasan Group, Inc.

Photography by Digital Studios, Austin, Texas and Park Street Photography with the following exceptions:

The stock agencies have been abbreviated as follows.

AA: Animals Animals; C: Corbis; GH: Grant Heilman Photography, Inc.; IW: The Image Works; PE: PhotoEdit; PR: Photo Researchers; SB: Stock Boston; SM: The Stock Market; SS: Superstock; TI: Tony Stone International; UN: Uniphoto; US: Unicorn Stock Photos;

(ant) © Runk/Schoenberger/GH; (baby) © SS; (band) © Mary Kate Denny/PE; (beak) © Arthur Smith III/GH; (bear) © Runk/Schoenberger/GH; (beard) © Brenda Tharp/PR; (bee) © Stephen Dalton/AA; (boy) © Tony Latham/TI; (bridge) © UN; (camel) © PhotoDisc; (chandelier) © SS; (chauffeur) © Pete Saloutos/SM; (cheer) © Myrleen Ferguson/PE; (chef) © Doug Martin/PR; (chemist) © Dennis O'Clair/TI; (child) © Jon Feingersh/SM; (chimney) © Tony Freeman/PE; (city) © SS; (claw) © Tom McHugh/PR; (clown) © SS; (cow) © Gi Bernard/AA; (couple) © SS; (crab) © Bruce Forster/TI; (crash) © Kenneth L. Miller/UN; (crawl) © Myrleen Ferguson/PE; (crew) © Jeff Zaruba/SM; (crow) © Peter Saloutous/SM; (crowd) © Chuck Savage/SM; (elephant) © James Balog/TI; (engine) © Berle Chemey/UN; (field) © John Strawser/GH; (fight) © David Young-Wolff/PE; (fly) © Donald Specker/AA; (fox) © Darrell Fulin/TI; (gate) © Robert W. Ginn/US; (gerbil) © Robert Maier/AA; (gold) © T. Tracey/FPG; (harp) © Richard Gross/SM; (haul) © Jr. Williams/Earth Scenes; (hawk) © PhotoDisc; (hay) © Tony Craddock/TI; (iump) © David Young-Wolff/PE; (kangaroo) © PhotoDisc; (man) © SS;

(mare) © Robert Maier/AA; (men) © UN; (mew) © Robert Haddocks/TI; (mouse) © J. M. Labat/Jacana/PR; (mow) © David Frazier/PR; (noise) © Michael Newman/PE; (nose) © UN; (nurse) ATC Productions/SM; (orchestra) © Tony Freeman/PE; (orchid) © Charles Marden Fitch/SS; (ox) © Russell Grunake/US; (parachute) © SS; (point) © Michael Newman/PE; (post) © Michael Habicht/Earth Scenes; (rabbit) © PhotoDisc; (rowboat) © Margaret Kios/SM; (scream) © Chris Collins/SM; (sea) © Bob Abraham/SM; (shark) © W. Gregory Brown/AA; (sheep) © Tim Davis/PR; (shield) © SS; (shrimp) © AA; (shrub) © Wes Thompson/SM (sleep) © Myrleen Ferguson/PE; (sleigh) © Guy Gillette/PR; (slide) © Michael Newman/PE; (smile) © SS; (smoke) © Barry Rowland/TI; (snake) © PhotoDisc; (snowflake) © Gerben Oppermans/TI; (splash) © Ray Massey/TI; (squirrel) © Laurie Campbell/TI; (stage) © Bob Gomel/SM; (strong) © Gerard Vandystadt/PR; (swim) © Kathy Ferguson/PE; (them) © Rob Lewine/SM; (throat) © Jeff Greenberg/US; (tree) © Rich Iwasaki/TI; (twins) © Chip Henderson/TI; (vault) © SS (wall) © Leslie Borden/PE; (wasp) © Stephen Dalton/AA; (wave) © Warren Bolster/TI; (well) © Amy C. Etra/PE; (whale) © Gerald Lim/US; (wheat) © Kevin R. Morris/TI; (yawn) © Aneal Vohra/US; (zoo) © John M. Roberts/SM.

Additional Photography: p. 5 © Spencer Grant/PhotoEdit (boy); © PhotoDisc Inc. (rooster); p. 27 © Steve Dunwell/The Image Bank (city snowfall); © Calvin Larsen/Photo Researchers (bus); © PhotoDisc Inc. (traffic light, meter, one-way sign, stop sign, taxi); p. 39 © Bob Thomason/Tony Stone Images; p. 41 © Corel Corp.; p. 43 © John Elk III/Bruce Coleman, Inc.; p. 45 © Peter Pearson/Tony Stone Images; p. 49 © Ken Biggs/Tony Stone Images (Houston); © Gary Taylor/Tony Stone Images (Dallas); p. 51 Hugh Sitton/Tony Stone Images; p. 55 © Paul McCormick/The Image Bank (bear with cub, eagle); © MetaTools, Inc. (butterfly); p. 62 © David David Gallery/Superstock (antelope painting; mesa painting; © Christie's, London/Superstock (coast painting); p. 67 © UNIPHOTO; p. 68 © COMSTOCK (boy on sled); © T.F. Chen/Superstock (girls playing soccer); p. 71 © Jeff Lepore; p. 78 © Gary Neil Corbett/Superstock (poison ivy); © Joy & Roger Spurr/Bruce Coleman, Inc. (poison oak, poison sumac); p. 82 © Superstock, Inc.; p. 85 © Norman Owen Tomalin/Bruce Coleman, Inc. (main); © Dean Krakel II/Photo Researchers (spot); p. 89 © Cathlyn Melloan/Tony Stone Images (dinosaur); © Sinclair Stammers/Photo Researchers (fossil); © PhotoDisc Inc. (chest); © Metatools, Inc. (dinosaur) p. 94 © Mercury Archive/The Image Bank; p. 96 © Mary Evans Picture Library/Photo Researchers; p. 97 © Ron Dahlquist/Superstock; p. 106 © PhotoDisc Inc.; p. 108 © Superstock, Inc.; p. 111 © The Bridgeman Art Library, London/Superstock; p. 114 © Vanessa Vick/Photo Researchers (mask); © Jacksonville Art Museum, Florida/Superstock (sculpture); © Francois Gohier/Photo Researchers (Indian paintings); p. 115 © Superstock, Inc.; p. 117 © Egyptian National Museum, Cairo/Superstock (Tut's mask); © D. Heoclin/Gamma-Liasion Network (Tut's jewelry); p. 118 © George Holton/Photo Researchers (Tut's coffin); © J. Polleross/The Stock Market (Tut's treasures); p. 121 © Nuridsany et Pérennou/Photo Researchers (spider); p. 123 © A.H. Rider/Photo Researchers (ant); © PhotoDisc Inc. (orange, grapes); p. 125 © Corel Corp.; p. 129 © E.R. Degginger/Photo Researchers; p. 133 © Margarette Mead/The Image Bank (frog); © Will Crocker/The Image Bank (snake); p. 134 © Superstock, Inc. (bears); © Stephen Krasemann/Photo Researchers (baboons); p. 135 © David Young-Wolff/PhotoEdit; p. 136 © PhotoDisc Inc.; p. 138 © Steinhart Aquarium/Photo Researchers; p. 139 © PhotoDisc Inc. (penguins, ostrich); p. 144 © Superstock, Inc.; p. 146 © George Holton/Photo Researchers; p. 149 © D. Heoclin/Gamma-Liasion Network (grasshopper in trap); © Scott Camazine/Photo Researchers (spider); p. 151 © Simon D. Pollard/Photo Researchers (stalk-eyed fly); © Superstock, Inc. (assassin fly); © PhotoDisc Inc. (Long-horned beetle, jewel beetle, true bug); p. 152 © Penelope Breese/Gamma-Liaison Network; p. 154 © D. Redfearn/The Image Bank (cat); p. 157 © Tim Flach/Tony Stone Images; p. 161 © Richard Heinzen/Superstock (girls reading); © Metatools, Inc. (computer); © PhotoDisc Inc. (film reel); p. 165 © PhotoDisc Inc.; p. 174 © PhotoDisc Inc.; p. 181 © Corel Corp.; p. 182 © PhotoDisc Inc.; p. 185 © Superstock, Inc.; p. 186 PhotoDisc Inc. (collage); © MetaTools, Inc. (gazette).

The Sand-Man

I know a man
With a face of tan
But who is ever kind;
Whom girls and boys
Leave games and toys
Each eventide to find.

When day grows dim,
They watch for him,
He comes to place his claim;
He wears a crown
Of Dreaming-town;
The sand-man is his name.

When sparkling eyes
Troop sleepywise
And busy lips grow dumb;
When little heads
Nod toward the beds,
We know the sand-man's come.

Paul Laurence Dunbar

Think About It

Why is sleep called the sand-man?
Why is sleep important to a healthy life?

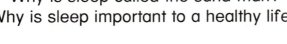

5

Dear Family of _____,

Your child will be learning about short and long vowel sounds. Your child will be using these skills to read about the theme of Day and Night. Here are some activities you can do together.

- Help your child make a list of things that are associated with day and night, such as *sun* or *moon*. Have your child draw a circle around any words with a short vowel sound and draw a box around any words with a long vowel sound.

- Make a chart of your family members' names. Change each name by changing the vowel to another long or short vowel sound. Complete the chart with a variety of names. Then have fun by calling each other by your new names for a day or two.

Name	Short Vowel	Long Vowel
Mom	Mim	
Dad		Dude
James		Jomes
Todd	Tadd	
Kate		Kite

- Make a long and short vowel bingo grid similar to the one shown. Then gather ten small items from around the house whose names have long and short vowel sounds, such as *pen, clip, game,* or *dime*. Put these items in a bag. Pick an item from the bag and say its name. Have your child write the word on the bingo grid in the correct square.

Vowel Bingo

long a	short u	long i dime
short e pen	Free	short i
long o	Free	long e
short o	long u	short a

LIBRARY LINK

You might like to visit the library and find the book *Fly By Night* by June Crebbin. Read it with your child.

Estimada familia de _____,

Su niño o niña aprenderá los sonidos en inglés de las vocales llamadas "cortas" y "largas". Usará estos conocimientos en su lectura acerca de El día y la noche. Algunas actividades que usted y su niño o niña pueden hacer en inglés aparecen a continuación.

- Ayude a su niño o niña a hacer una lista de cosas relacionadas con el día y la noche, tales como *sun* y *moon*. Pida a su niño o niña que dibuje un círculo alrededor de las palabras con el sonido de una vocal "corta" y que dibuje un cuadro alrededor de las palabras con el sonido de una vocal "larga".

- Hagan una gráfica con los nombres de los miembros de la familia. Véase la gráfica que aparece arriba. Cambien las vocales "largas" o "cortas" de cada nombre por otras vocales "largas" o "cortas." Completen la gráfica con una variedad de nombres. Luego, diviértanse por uno o dos días llamándose unos a otros con los nuevos nombres.

- Construyan una gráfica de bingo de vocales "largas" y "cortas" como la que aparece arriba. Luego, coleccionen diez objetos que encuentren por la casa y cuyos nombres tengan los sonidos de vocales "largas" y "cortas", como *pen, clip, game* o *dime*. Pongan estos objetos en una bolsa. Saque uno de la bolsa y diga su nombre. Pídale a su niño o niña que escriba la palabra en la gráfica de bingo en el cuadro correcto.

map   **bed**   **fish**   **fox**   **cup**

Write the picture names in the correct columns.

RULE If a word has only one vowel, the vowel sound is usually short.

Short a	Short e	Short i	Short o	Short u
_____	_____	_____	_____	_____
_____	_____	_____	_____	_____
_____	_____	_____	_____	_____

1. mop
2. bag
3. men
4. ant
5. egg
6. van
7. bus
8. inch
9. sun
10. six
11. ox
12. rug
13. ten
14. box
15. pig

Name _____

> **Circle the word that completes each sentence.
> Write the word on the line.**

1. When I wake up, I see the _____.   set   sun   sit

2. On Saturday morning, I _____ in the garden.   help   heap   hello

3. I wear a _____ to keep the sun off my head.   heat   hen   hat

4. I take care of all my _____.   please   plugs   plants

5. I _____ my bucket with water.   five   fill   fall

6. I water the plants and _____ out the weeds.   dig   drip   deep

7. About noon, it starts to get _____.   hot   hill   hit

8. I stop for a rest and sit on a _____.   pinch   bench   bean

9. I watch a lizard jump on a _____.   rock   road   rack

10. I see a black _____ crawl by.   big   bug   bag

11. I wish a little frog would _____ by, too.   hog   hop   hope

12. The morning is at an _____.   elf   mend   end

13. I'll go in and eat my _____ now.   lunch   lamp   lurch

14. This is the _____ way to spend time in the sun!   bus   best   beet

15. I _____ that I could go to the garden every day.   push   wish   wash

Ask your child to find words in the sentences that have short vowels.

rake kite smoke

Write each picture name on the line.

1 5
_____

2
_____

3
_____

4
_____

5
_____

6
_____

7
_____

8
_____

Complete each sentence with a word from the box.

9. Each morning, I try to _____ up at the same time.

10. I don't like to be _____ for school.

11. In fact, I pride myself on being on _____.

12. It takes me _____ minutes to wake up.

13. I eat breakfast in my _____.

14. Sometimes I drink a _____ carton of milk.

15. Then I _____ a quick bath.

16. After I'm dressed, I _____ my bed.

17. On some days, I walk a _____ to school.

18. On other days, I get a _____ with my neighbor.

five
late
make
mile
ride
robe
take
time
wake
whole

Name _____

bee

leaf

cube

Choose a word from the box to name each picture. Write the word on the line.

RULES When two vowels come together in a word, the first vowel usually has the long sound. The second vowel is silent. A vowel usually has the long sound when a consonant and **e** come after it.

| bee | feet |
| June | beak |

1. _____

2. _____

3. _____

| sea | cube |
| plume | tree |

4. _____

5. _____

6. _____

| tune | teeth |
| read | leaf |

7. _____

8. _____

9. _____

Complete each sentence with one of the words from the boxes above.

10. At night, I like to _____ books and articles about birds.

11. Did you know that birds do not have _____ in their mouths?

12. A bird uses its _____ to get food, but it does not chew.

13. Some birds cannot fly, so they get around on their _____.

14. The ostrich cannot fly, but it has a long _____ on its tail.

15. The month of _____ is a good time to watch birds.

16. The mockingbird sings a lovely _____ in the morning.

17. You can often see a bird's nest in a _____.

18. Birds that live near the _____ make their nests in other places.

AT HOME

Have your child write the headings **ee, ea,** and **u_e** on a piece of paper. Help your child find words on the page for each category.

nail   **hay**   **coat**   **hoe**   **key**   **tie**

Circle the picture name. Write it on the line. Underline the vowel that stands for the long sound. Put an X on the silent letter.

RULE When two vowels come together in a word, the first vowel usually has the long sound. The second vowel is silent.

1
bright
blue
beet

_____

2
day
drain
daisy

_____

3
keg
kite
key

_____

4
hoe
heel
how

_____

5
rail
rain
real

_____

6
dig
deep
die

_____

7
coal
coat
cube

_____

8
pal
peel
pail

_____

Complete each sentence with a word from the box.

9. Each day I like to _____ soccer.

10. It is _____ that millions of children play soccer.

11. Many kids can't _____ to join a soccer team.

12. A _____ teaches the players the rules of the game.

13. Learning to work with others is one of the _____ lessons.

14. The _____ to success is always trying to do your best.

15. It doesn't matter which team made the last _____.

16. Soccer is fun whether you win, lose, or _____.

coach
goal
key
main
play
tie
true
wait

Name _____

Complete each sentence with a word from the box.

1. At sunrise, the sun _____ to peek over the land.

2. All morning, the sun will _____ in the sky.

3. The sun is highest in the middle of the _____.

4. At noon, the sun is _____ overhead.

5. _____ in the day, the sun seems to slide down the sky.

6. Its _____ seem to get longer.

7. Finally, the sun sets, and its _____ fade.

8. This _____ the land dark and night comes.

9. The sun doesn't really _____ around the sky.

10. It stays in one _____.

11. The _____ to the sun's position is the movement of Earth.

12. Earth spins around once _____ day.

beams
day
each
key
late
leaves
place
rays
rise
roam
seems
straight

Ask your child to read some of the sentences to you and to point out the words with long vowels.

light **colt** **wind**

Circle the word that names the picture. Write the word on the line.

RULE Some words with only one vowel have the long sound instead of the short sound.

1

fight
fit
five
_____

2

chin
child
chilled
_____

3

nickel
nine
night
_____

4

fin
fine
find
_____

5

Mark Garza
1. gift 100%
2. rice
3. city
4. cent

right
ripe
rigid
_____

6

rope
rode
roll
_____

7

pose
post
pot
_____

8

goal
golf
gold
_____

9

grind
grill
grin
_____

Use a word from the box to answer each riddle.

10. Which word means the opposite of day? _____

11. Which word tells something you do to clothes? _____

12. Which word means to be good-hearted? _____

13. Which word tells about animals that roam free? _____

14. Which word tells what people do with babies? _____

15. Which word names something that can grow on bread? _____

| fold |
| hold |
| kind |
| might |
| mold |
| night |
| wild |

Name _____

Complete each sentence with a word from the box.

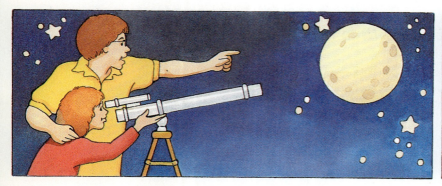  

| bright | find | high | hold | light | might | moldy |
| most | night | old | rind | sight | told | tonight |

1. Go outside on almost any _____.

2. _____ your head back.

3. What do you see up _____ in the sky?

4. The shining moon is a beautiful _____.

5. You _____ know that the moon does not make its own rays.

6. The _____ of the sun bounces off the moon and shines on Earth.

7. Many stories have been _____ about the moon.

8. One story tells that the moon is made of _____ green cheese.

9. Another is that you can see the face of an _____ man in the moon.

10. Watch for a few nights and you will _____ that the moon seems to change.

11. Sometimes, it looks like a big, _____ circle.

12. Other times it looks as thin as a watermelon _____.

13. The moon shines _____ nights, but sometimes it does not shine at all.

14. How do you think the moon will look _____?

 AT HOME

Have your child read the sentences. Look at and talk about the moon with your child.

dog = 1   rabbit = 2   elephant = 3

Write each word from the box below the number of syllables it has.

alphabet	beetle	envelope	flashlight	helmet
kangaroo	peacock	pie	rain	rice
team	triangle	valentine	vest	wheelchair

One Syllable	Two Syllables	Three Syllables
_____	_____	_____
_____	_____	_____
_____	_____	_____
_____	_____	_____
_____	_____	_____

Read each book title. Circle the words with two syllables. Write the words with three syllables.

1. *The Toothpaste Millionaire*   _____ _____

2. *Oh, Honestly, Angela!*   _____ _____

3. *Unreal! Eight Surprising Stories!*   _____ _____

4. *Superfudge*   _____ _____

5. *Otherwise Known as Sheila the Great*   _____ _____

6. *Paul's Volcano*   _____ _____

Name _____

Read each word. Write the number of vowels you see and the number of vowel sounds you hear. Then write the number of syllables the word has.

	Vowels You See	Vowels You Hear	Number of Syllables
1. bolt	——	——	——
2. coat	——	——	——
3. vase	——	——	——
4. sandwich	——	——	——
5. sweeping	——	——	——
6. feet	——	——	——
7. leaf	——	——	——
8. beautiful	——	——	——
9. blue	——	——	——
10. cabin	——	——	——

	Vowels You See	Vowels You Hear	Number of Syllables
11. citizen	——	——	——
12. submarine	——	——	——
13. tissue	——	——	——
14. magazine	——	——	——
15. paintbrush	——	——	——
16. grandmother	——	——	——
17. turkey	——	——	——
18. lawnmower	——	——	——
19. basketball	——	——	——
20. photograph	——	——	——

Read each sentence. Circle the words with two syllables. Write the words with three syllables.

21. Tonight, Beth's piano teacher is coming to dinner. _____

22. Beth made gingerbread cookies for dessert. _____

23. Later, Mack called Beth on the telephone. _____

24. "Do you understand the math homework?" Mack asked. _____

25. Mack was worried about the test tomorrow morning. _____

26. Before she went to bed, Beth read her favorite book. _____

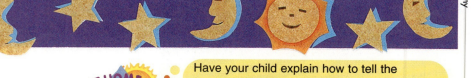

AT HOME

Have your child explain how to tell the number of syllables in a word.

fly   baby   gym

The words in the box are hidden in the puzzle. Circle each word you find. Words can go across or down. Then write each word in the correct column below.

c	y	c	l	e	f	i	f	t	y	h
y	z	a	b	u	s	y	g	m	b	y
l	d	p	j	g	s	p	y	y	u	d
i	j	p	e	n	n	y	m	t	d	r
n	v	l	l	k	c	r	y	h	d	a
d	r	y	l	w	p	a	r	t	y	n
e	x	d	y	n	a	m	i	t	e	t
r	j	a	l	g	l	i	l	y	q	b
s	y	s	t	e	m	d	o	p	f	f
h	e	u	t	y	p	i	c	a	l	d
b	o	c	y	m	b	a	l	m	p	y

apply	buddy	busy
cry	cycle	cylinder
cymbal	dry	dynamite
fifty	gym	hydrant
jelly	lily	myth
party	penny	pyramid
spy	system	typical

y as in **fly**

_____

_____

_____

_____

_____

_____

_____

y as in **baby**

_____

_____

_____

_____

_____

_____

_____

y as in **gym**

_____

_____

_____

_____

_____

_____

_____

Name _____

Use a word from the box to complete each sentence.

baby	baby-sit
crying	family
happy	history
lullaby	memory
poetry	rhyme
sleepy	story
system	typical

1. Throughout _____, people have sung babies to sleep.

2. It is still a _____ way of soothing children.

3. Many parents use this _____ at bedtime.

4. They might sing songs, say nursery rhymes, or read _____.

5. The type of song used to sing children to sleep is called a _____.

6. Some of these songs have characters and tell a _____.

7. Many of the songs have some words that _____.

8. A _____ child is often cranky.

9. Singing can soothe a weeping _____ or toddler.

10. After just a few minutes, many children will stop _____.

11. Soon the child will drift off to _____ sleep.

12. Remember this if you ever _____ a young child.

13. Many people have a sweet _____ of being sung to sleep.

14. Do you remember a _____ member singing to you at night?

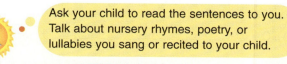

Ask your child to read the sentences to you. Talk about nursery rhymes, poetry, or lullabies you sang or recited to your child.

salad

Draw a line to match each picture to its name. Circle the vowel that stands for the **schwa** sound in each word.

1. camel

2. adult

3. lemon

4. cactus

5. gerbil

6. engine

7. carrots

8. circus

9. rocket

10. giant

Complete each sentence with a word from the box. Circle the vowel that stands for the **schwa** sound in each word you write.

11. Last Wednesday I had a _____ from school.

12. Dad and I planned a trip to the museum to see _____.

13. First, my _____ stopped at Mom's office.

14. Her building is _____ from the museum.

15. We went upstairs in an _____.

16. _____, it jerked to a stop.

17. Mom pushed a button and it set off an _____.

18. Soon workers found a _____ to restart the elevator.

19. When we got to the top, the _____ of the company was waiting.

20. We were fine, but we _____ that next time we'll take the stairs!

**across
agreed
alarm
elevator
family
fossils
holiday
method
president
suddenly**

Name _____

Read each word in the box and listen for the number of syllables. Then write each word in the correct column at the right. Circle the vowel that stands for the schwa sound in each word you write.

across
antenna
automatic
diagram
diet
magazine
scientific
variety
zebra

Two Syllables	Three Syllables	Four Syllables
_____	_____	_____
_____	_____	_____
_____	_____	_____

Rewrite each word on the line, drawing lines to divide each into syllables. Circle the vowels that stand for the schwa sound.

1. principal _____

2. elephant _____

3. arithmetic _____

4. apron _____

5. similar _____

6. identify _____

7. canopy _____

8. idea _____

9. marathon _____

10. easily _____

11. symphony _____

AT HOME

Help your child write a list of words with two or more syllables. Have your child circle the vowels that stand for the **schwa** sound.

© Steck-Vaughn Company

In each of these sentences, the word **night** stands for one of the spelling words in the box. Write the correct word on the line.

PHONICS and SPELLING

across	beam	beep	bolt	busy	chain
city	coat	day	due	high	lit
money	place	shine	sleep	try	wait

1. A night at night is different from during the day.

2. During the night, people rush around.

3. They dart in buildings and night right back out again.

4. In the day, people shout and cars night their horns.

5. Everyone is trying to work and earn night.

6. At night, things are not as night.

7. Think of it as the city dressing in her black night .

8. The darkness seems to spill night the streets.

9. The sun is down, but lights night all around.

10. Street lamps gleam from up night.

11. A few windows in buildings are night up.

12. Cars drive along as their lights night in front of them.

13. A few people walk from one night to another.

14. Most are resting at home, getting ready to night.

15. The darkness just seems to night for morning to come.

16. It is a night of events that is repeated day in and day out.

17. Every morning, the sun is night to chase away the dark.

18. Every night, the dark will night to quiet and calm the day.

1. _____ 2. _____ 3. _____ 4. _____

5. _____ 6. _____ 7. _____ 8. _____

9. _____ 10. _____ 11. _____ 12. _____

13. _____ 14. _____ 15. _____ 16. _____

17. _____ 18. _____

Name _____

Follow the directions to read the messages.

For each box:

1. Cross out all the words with three syllables.

2. Cross out all the words with the schwa sound.

3. Cross out all the words with a short vowel sound.

4. Starting at the bottom right corner and working backward, bottom to top, write the remaining words to form a message.

wonderful	day	man	each	animal	emptiness	fit	duck
understand	with	majesty	brightly	club	fun	about	
ribbon	smiling	umbrella	circus	try	pupil	whatever	

_____

_____

pyramid	tree	that	my	hand	important	by
win	outside	majesty	path	celebrate	meal	suddenly
noon	awhile	your	powerful	eat	hill	melon

_____

_____

crocodile	balance	bright	up	day	sun	see	luxury
you'll	symbol	autobus	grocery	history	bat	soon	sofa
tight	adult	sleep	salad	night	pencil	good	company	dip

_____

_____

AT HOME

Have your child put the puzzle words he or she crossed out in the correct categories.

Read the passage. Then answer the questions below.

PHONICS and READING

Places in Time

What time is it right now? For you it is daytime, but for those on the other side of the globe it is deep night. The moon shines and stars twinkle in the sky. People lie in bed asleep. In another place, the sun rises and people wake up. They eat breakfast. They dress for work and for school. Somewhere else, families eat their evening meals. The sun is setting. How can this be?

The sun's light shines on one half of Earth at a time. It is day in part of the world and night in another part.

The nations of the world have agreed on a system to measure time. Earth is divided into areas called "time zones." There are 24 time zones, just as there are 24 hours in a day. All the places within a time zone share the same time. When you move from one time zone to the next, the time changes by one hour. If you travel east to the next time zone, the time will be one hour later. If you travel west to the next time zone, the time will be one hour earlier. At the same time, in two different places in the world, friends are saying "good morning" or "good night."

1. Why is it possible for it to be night in one part of the world and day in another?

_____

2. What is the system nations use to measure time?

_____

3. What can be said about the time within one time zone?

_____

4. What happens as you travel from one time zone to the next?

_____

Name _____

What is your favorite time of day? Write a paragraph about it. Describe how it looks outside, tell what you usually do, and explain why you like this time best. The words in the box may help you.

PHONICS and WRITING

across	afternoon	beam	beautiful	busy
easily	family	light	lullaby	lunch
pretty	ray	sleep	tonight	typical

_____

_____

WRITING TIP Before you begin, make a list of your ideas.

_____

_____

_____

_____

_____

_____

_____

_____

_____

AT HOME

Have your child read the paragraph to you.

Circle the picture name. Write the word on the line.

1

keep
key
kite

_____

2

dime
day
die

_____

3

fight
fright
fit

_____

4

cub
cry
cube

_____

5
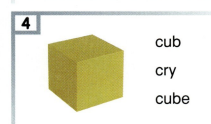
hoe
hole
hive

_____

6

gleam
glue
gray

_____

7

cyclone
candy
cymbals

_____

8

rain
ray
rod

_____

9

win
wind
whine

_____

Circle the vowel or vowels that stand for the schwa sound in each word. Then write the number of syllables on the line.

10. alphabet _____

11. scientific _____

12. lesson _____

13. umbrella _____

14. similar _____

15. oxygen _____

16. idea _____

17. canopy _____

18. walrus _____

19. marathon _____

20. valentine _____

21. realize _____

22. automatic _____

23. holiday _____

24. arrive _____

Name _____

Fill in the circle next the word that completes each sentence.

1. The moon and the stars come out at _____.
   - ○ next
   - ○ night
   - ○ nickel
   - ○ nose

2. My grandmother knows all about my family's _____.
   - ○ suddenly
   - ○ straight
   - ○ history
   - ○ each

3. The word *animal* has _____ syllables.
   - ○ three
   - ○ five
   - ○ two
   - ○ six

4. My mom gave me some _____ to buy a book.
   - ○ may
   - ○ mail
   - ○ money
   - ○ meat

5. When is that homework _____?
   - ○ day
   - ○ die
   - ○ deep
   - ○ due

6. A paper towel tube is a _____.
   - ○ cylinder
   - ○ cycle
   - ○ city
   - ○ cry

7. On a _____ day, we learn many new things.
   - ○ try
   - ○ tonight
   - ○ triangle
   - ○ typical

8. Look at the beautiful _____ of sunlight!
   - ○ ripe
   - ○ reach
   - ○ rain
   - ○ ray

9. Is it important for all poems to _____?
   - ○ rhyme
   - ○ reply
   - ○ rate
   - ○ rip

10. The weather may get very _____ today.
    - ○ can
    - ○ cold
    - ○ coat
    - ○ cone

11. Please turn off the hall _____ when you leave.
    - ○ leak
    - ○ light
    - ○ line
    - ○ lone

12. The _____ of time zones is used to measure time.
    - ○ system
    - ○ seat
    - ○ seal
    - ○ send

It Fell in the City

It fell in the city,
It fell through the night,
And the black rooftops
All turned white.

Red fire hydrants
All turned white.
Blue police cars
All turned white.

Green garbage cans
All turned white.
Gray sidewalks
All turned white.

Yellow NO PARKING signs
All turned white.
When it fell in the city
All through the night.

Eve Merriam

Think About It

Why did police cars all turn white?
What else might change in the city when this happens?

Dear Family of _____,

Your child will be learning about variant consonant sounds, such as *g* in *page* and *peg*, consonant blends, such as *sch* in *school*, consonant digraphs, such as *thr* in *thread*, and silent letters such as *kn* in *knife*. Your child will be using these skills to read about the theme of Cities. Here are some activities you can do together.

- Choose a short article from the newspaper. Ask your child to circle any words that contain initial consonant blends, such as *president*, *twenty*, or *space*. Then have your child sort the words into three lists: words with one syllable, words with two syllables, and words with three syllables.

- Write one word that contains a silent letter, such as *knife*, *wrench*, *thumb*, *guide*, *laugh*, *whale*, or *science*. Take turns with your child adding new words. Each new word must use one letter from a previous word, as shown here.

- Make a spinner, using cardboard and a paper clip, like the one shown here. Spin the spinner. When it stops, say a word that has the same sound as the digraph letters on the game. The digraph can be at the beginning of the word (shoe) or at the end of the word (beach).

LIBRARY LINK

You might like to visit the library and find the book *The Adventures of Taxi Dog* by Debra Barracca. Read it with your child.

Estimada familia de _____,

Su niño o niña aprenderá los sonidos variantes de algunas consonantes en inglés, tales como la *g* en *page* y *peg*; combinaciones de consonantes, tales como *sch* en *school*, *thr* en *thread*; además de consonantes "silenciosas" como *kn* en *knife*. Su niño o niña usará estos conocimientos en su lectura sobre Las ciudades. Algunas actividades que usted y su niño o niña pueden hacer en inglés aparecen a continuación.

- Elija un artículo corto de un periódico. Pídale a su niño o niña que dibuje un círculo alrededor de las palabras que tengan combinaciones de consonantes iniciales, como *president*, *twenty* o *space*. Luego, pídale a su niño o niña que separe las palabras en tres listas: las palabras de una sola sílaba, las palabras de dos sílabas y las palabras de tres sílabas.

- Escriba una palabra que tenga una letra "silenciosa", como *knife*, *wrench*, *thumb*, *guide*, *laugh*, *whale* o *science*. Túrnense añadiendo palabras nuevas. Cada palabra nueva debe usar una letra de la palabra anterior, como se demuestra arriba.

- Construya una rueda con una aguja giratoria usando un pedazo de cartón y un sujetapapeles como aparece más arriba. Haga girar la aguja. Cuando pare, diga una palabra que tenga el mismo sonido de la combinación de consonantes que indica la aguja. Estas consonantes pueden ser iniciales en la palabra (shoe) o finales en la palabra (beach).

The words in the box are hidden in the puzzle. Circle each word you find. Words can go across, down, or diagonally. Then write each word under the correct heading for the sound.

ace	camera	canoe	cap	celery
cents	corner	police	race	traffic

soft c in city

_____

_____

_____

_____

_____

t	u	p	o	l	i	c	e
m	c	b	o	c	b	e	t
d	r	a	c	e	g	n	r
a	c	e	m	l	y	t	a
c	o	r	n	e	r	s	f
o	a	v	j	r	r	p	f
h	n	p	o	y	z	a	i
i	c	a	n	o	e	b	c

hard c in cat

_____

_____

_____

_____

_____

Read the passage. Complete the sentences with words from the lists above.

Carla was on her way to the city market on the _____. She had

one dollar and fifty _____. Her mom wanted her to get some

_____ for dinner.

At the crosswalk, a _____ officer held up her hand. She stopped

_____ so Carla could cross the street. Carla saw a man using a

_____. She also saw a lot of runners having a _____.

Name _____

Say each word in the box. Then write each word under the correct heading below.

badge	bag	cages	engine	fudge	game
gerbil	giraffe	goat	gorilla	grill	guests
gusty	gym	jungle	large	orange	sugar

soft g in giraffe   **hard g in gas**

_____   _____

_____   _____

_____   _____

_____   _____

_____   _____

_____   _____

_____   _____

_____   _____

_____   _____

Complete each sentence with a word from the lists above.

1. At the Bronx Zoo, the animals do not live in _____.

2. They live in _____ areas called habitats.

3. You might see a tall _____ whose neck reaches up into the trees.

4. You might see a big, silverback _____ lounging under a tree.

5. One habitat looks like a _____ or rain forest.

6. At the Children's Zoo, you can pet a kid or a full-grown _____.

7. You can eat a snack of _____ or popcorn at the zoo.

8. The _____ put their empty containers in a trash can.

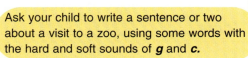

Ask your child to write a sentence or two about a visit to a zoo, using some words with the hard and soft sounds of **g** and **c.**

sock

rose

sugar

tissue

Read each word and listen for the sound the letter s stands for. Write s, z, or sh to show which sound you hear.

RULE The letter **s** can stand for the **s** sound heard in **sock**, the **z** sound heard in **rose**, and the **sh** sound heard in **sugar** and **tissue**.

1. assure _____
2. cheese _____
3. class _____
4. hose _____
5. insect _____
6. insurance _____
7. issue _____
8. please _____
9. present _____
10. pressure _____
11. secret _____
12. softball _____
13. summer _____
14. sure _____
15. tissue _____

Answer each riddle with a word from the list above.

16. Almost every city has a field on which to play me.

    I'm a summer pastime. What am I? _____

17. I'm the warmest season of the year.

    What am I? _____

18. Use me when you have a cold. Don't sneeze

    without me! What am I? _____

19. Use me to water the garden. Firefighters use me

    to put out fires. What am I? _____

20. I am the opposite of maybe. I'm certain of it.

    What am I? _____

21. I am yellow and am good to eat. I can be Swiss

    or cheddar. What am I? _____

22. I'm something you want to keep to yourself.

    Don't tell me! What am I? _____

Name _____

Read the passage. Complete the sentences with words from the box.

cabbage	center	city	corner	daisies	ensure	gate
hose	large	site	soil	squash	sure	vegetables

Cindy and Gerry live in a high-rise building in a big _____. Near their

building is a _____ park. A city garden is in one _____ of

the park. A white fence with an orange _____ keeps animals out of the

garden. Many families have plots of _____ in the garden. They share a

_____ for watering, and they share other garden tools.

Cindy likes to plant _____, such as lettuce and celery. In the spring,

she plants broccoli, carrots, and leafy vegetables, such as _____. Late in

the summer, she waits for autumn plants, such as acorn _____, to ripen.

By September, her family is _____ to enjoy Cindy's harvest.

Gerry has the _____ next to Cindy's. Gerry enjoys flowers, so he

plants pansies, _____, lilies, and roses. At the _____

of Gerry's garden, he plants sunflowers. Gerry puts plant food on his flowers to

_____ that they will bloom.

Unit 2: Reading Variant Sounds
for *c, g,* and *s* in Context

AT HOME

Ask your child to point out and read other
words in this passage that have the variant
sounds for *c, g,* and *s*.

skate

Write a two-letter **s** blend to complete each word.

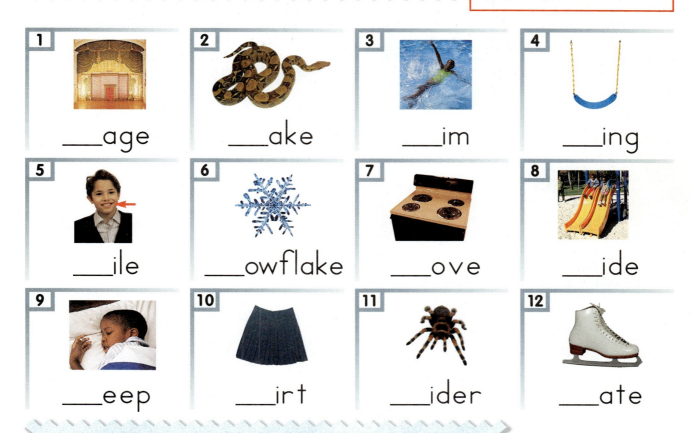

1. ___age

2. ___ake

3. ___im

4. ___ing

5. ___ile

6. ___owflake

7. ___ove

8. ___ide

9. ___eep

10. ___irt

11. ___ider

12. ___ate

Complete each sentence with a word from above.

13. Each winter, we go to the city ice rink to _____.

14. My sister has a skating outfit with tights and a short _____.

15. It is fun to _____ and glide on the ice.

16. We all join hands and skate in a line, like a long _____.

17. Sometimes we _____ each other around.

18. When it snows, we have fun chasing a _____ or two.

19. There is a little _____ near the ice that keeps us warm.

20. Skating is sure to bring a _____ to my face.

Name _____

string

Use a word from the box to name each picture. Write the word on the line. Then circle the three-letter blend in each word.

scrub	splash	split	spring	squirrel	straw	stripe	strong

1 _____

2 _____

3 _____

4 _____

5 _____

6 _____

7 _____

8 _____

Read each clue. Write a word from above to complete each row of the puzzle. Then read down the dark squares to answer the question below.

9. You drink through this.

10. Do this to logs to make firewood.

11. a small woodland or city animal

12. A skunk has a white one.

13. This is coiled and bouncy.

14. the opposite of *weak*

What kind of race is short and very fast?

_____

AT HOME

Have your child read the words in the puzzle and identify the three consonants that blend together in each word.

bridge

Read the first word in each box. Then make new words that match the clues. Change one letter at a time to make a new word.

1   **drip**

_____ to fall

_____ a harvest

_____ a black bird

2   **brain**

_____ to empty

_____ a locomotive

_____ a path

3   **crab**

_____ to take

_____ dull

_____ to pull

4   **trap**

_____ to stumble

_____ to grasp

_____ gloomy

5   **grape**

_____ grillwork

_____ a wooden box

_____ a heavy lifter

6   **truck**

_____ train rails

_____ to break

_____ a sharp noise

Read the passage. Complete each sentence with a word from the box.

crane   crash   crew   dream   drill   grass   trace   trucks

    I had a funny _____ last night. Two big _____ pulled up in front of the building across the street. One truck had a large black ball swinging from a _____. A worker used a noisy _____ to tear up the sidewalk. Then I heard a loud _____ that woke me up.

    I went to the window and saw a construction _____ working. It was not a dream! Not a _____ of the building across the street was left standing. I hope they put a park there and plant a lot of _____ and trees.

Name _____

flag

twelve

Unscramble the letters to make a word that names each picture.

1		swint	2		clobk	3		kalef
		_____			_____			_____
4		gwit	5		lepan	6		pesel
		_____			_____			_____

Read the passage. Complete the sentences with words from the box.

clear
flown
fly
glad
place
plane
please
twice
twilight
twinkling

John traveled to Paris to see his aunt and uncle. He lived in London,

so he wanted to _____ to Paris.

At the airport, he stood in line to get on the _____.

He asked the pilot, "May I _____ see the cockpit?"

The pilot said, "Have you ever _____ on a plane before?"

John said "Yes, I've flown _____, but I've never

seen the _____ where all the controls are." The

pilot was _____ to show where she worked. John

was amazed at all the _____ dials.

The sky was _____ as the plane neared Paris.

John liked to see Paris sparkle in the _____.

Unit 2: Initial Consonant Blends with
l and **tw**

AT HOME

Ask your child to make a list of words with
l blends.

lamp

Write each picture name on the first line. Write two more words from the box that end with the same consonant blend.

bald	blast	bolt	camp	clasp	dent	desk	grasp	land
limp	list	loft	melt	mild	raft	risk	went	wind

1 _____ _____ _____

2 _____ _____ _____

3 _____ _____ _____

4 _____ _____ _____

5 _____ _____ _____

6 _____ _____ _____

7 _____ _____ _____

8 _____ _____ _____

9 _____ _____ _____

Circle the word that completes each sentence. Write the word.

10. You can find many insects on the _____ in a city park.　　ground　grant

11. Look at that _____ where the old tree was.　stomp　stump

12. Hundreds of _____ live here!　ants　ask

13. They are having a delicious _____.　feats　feast

14. I _____ my father to look for insects with me.　wall　want

15. I will _____ him if he will look with me tonight.　asp　ask

Name _____

Read each word in the box and listen for the number of syllables you hear. Write each word under the correct heading.

blanket	brave	clock	flag	flashlight	frequent
grandfather	grasshopper	planet	president	prevent	probably
screen	skeleton	specific	spell	squint	traffic

One Syllable	Two Syllables	Three Syllables
_____	_____	_____
_____	_____	_____
_____	_____	_____
_____	_____	_____
_____	_____	_____
_____	_____	_____

Read the sentences. Circle each word that names a city, state, or country. If the circled word has two syllables, write it below.

1. Visit Moscow, Russia, if you like snowy winters.

2. You can get good Cuban food in Tampa, Florida.

3. People say that summers are great in Montreal, Canada.

4. In 1996, the Summer Olympics were held in Atlanta.

5. Scranton, Pennsylvania, is east of Cleveland, Ohio.

6. In Spain, Madrid is about three hundred miles from Barcelona.

Map © by Rand McNally R.L. #98-S-130

_____   _____

_____   _____

_____   _____

Study a map with your child to find place names with one, two, and three syllables.

knot

Read the clues. Use words from the box to complete the puzzle.

climb	ghost	gnat	guitar	knees	night	rhyme
scenic	signs	talked	thumb	wreck	wrench	write

Across

1. an accident

3. joints in your legs

6. a make-believe thing

7. one of your fingers

Down

1. a tool plumbers use

2. a tiny insect

4. an instrument with six strings

5. Many poems do this.

Read the passage. Complete the sentences with words from the box above.

My sister ———————— us into walking up the hill to Coit

Tower in San Francisco. The ———————— was so steep that

my mom said her ———————— might buckle. My dad joked

that he was going to stick out his ———————— and get a ride

the rest of the way. When we finally got to the tower, we followed

the ———————— to the elevator. We had a ————————

view of the city from the top of the tower. We watched the lights

come on as ———————— fell. I bought a postcard so I could

———————— this note!

Coit Tower

Name _____

**Complete each sentence with a word from the box.
Then circle the silent letter or letters in the word.**

climb	guard	guess	guide	guitar
Island	knew	knows	rhythm	right
scenic	scientists	sign	Tomb	wrong

1. A _____ took us on a tour of New York City.

2. A guide is someone who _____ the city well.

3. We saw a _____ that said, "Museum of Natural History."

4. This museum was created by many _____.

5. Then we visited Grant's _____, where U. S. Grant is buried.

6. We passed a musician who was playing a _____.

7. The musician had a steady _____ as she strummed.

8. The guide asked us to _____ where we would go next.

9. I suggested that we turn _____ at the next corner.

10. I _____ that Central Park was in that direction.

11. "No, you guessed _____," our guide said.

12. Instead we got on a boat for a _____ harbor tour.

13. The boat stopped at Liberty _____.

14. We decided to _____ the stairs of the Statue of Liberty.

15. A _____ there pointed out the World Trade Center.

AT HOME

Ask your child to name a city he or she would like to visit and to explain why.

© Steck-Vaughn Company

Read the article. Write complete sentences to answer the questions below.

PHONICS and READING

Toronto

Canada's largest city, Toronto, is located on the northwest shore of Lake Ontario. It is the capital of the province of Ontario. The name Toronto is a Huron Indian word that means "place of meeting." In the 1700s, Toronto was on the Indians' overland route between Lake Ontario and Lake Huron.

Today, Toronto is still a busy meeting place. It is a port city with many manufacturing companies that bring goods in and out. Toronto also has huge financial and communication centers. About two million people live in the greater Toronto area. Over 80 ethnic groups live there, and over 100 different languages are spoken in Toronto. For this reason, the United Nations named Toronto the world's most diverse city.

Toronto's diverse population makes it a very lively city. Toronto is home to the world's tallest free-standing tower, the world's third largest theater center, and 5,000 restaurants. It is also home to fine museums, shopping centers, and numerous sports teams. Toronto is one of the world's most exciting cities.

Toronto skyline from the harbor

1. Why did the Huron Indians name the area "Toronto"?

_____

2. Why is Toronto called the world's most diverse city?

_____

3. What is a port city?

_____

4. What brings worldwide recognition to Toronto?

_____

5. Name some activities people can do in Toronto.

_____

Name _____

Think of a city you know about, or one you would like to visit. Imagine you are a guide giving a tour of this city. Write about some of the places you would see on your tour. The words in the box may help you.

PHONICS and WRITING

between	block	center	climb	gold
grass	guest	island	know	large
statue	street	sure	train	twinkle

Writing Tip Decide on a city and discuss your writing ideas with a small group of classmates.

AT HOME • Have your child read the story to you.

chair

Say each picture name. Write the name if it begins with the same consonant digraph as the word at the left. Use the words in the box to help you.

chalk	Charles	chimney	churches	sheep	shell	ships
shore	Theater	thirteen	thumb	wheat	wheel	where

1

what

_____ _____ _____

2

she

_____ _____ _____

3

thing

13 _____ _____ _____

4

child

_____ _____ _____

Complete each sentence with a word from the box above.

5. Charleston, South Carolina, is a port on the Atlantic _____.

6. It was named for King _____ II of England in 1670.

7. _____ from all over the world deliver cargo to the city's docks.

8. Charleston is a place _____ history is alive.

9. It has many beautiful old homes and _____.

10. You can still see a play at the Dock Street _____, which was built in 1736.

Charleston, SC

Name _____

brush

Write a word from the box to match each clue. Then circle each word in the puzzle. Words can go down, across, or diagonally.

RULE Some words end with a **consonant digraph**.
bru**sh**   ba**th**   ma**tch**
sti**ck**   ri**ng**

1. A bird needs these to fly. _____

2. A chimney is often made of this. _____

3. You chew with these. _____

4. Use this to make your hair neat. _____

5. This is a fuzzy fruit. _____

6. This is a season. _____

7. Your shirt is made of this. _____

8. This can tell you the time. _____

9. This is something to sing. _____

brick	brush	bunch
cloth	leash	peach
search	song	spring
teeth	things	truck
watch	wings	with

s	w	a	t	c	h	s	b	o	p
b	r	u	s	h	x	p	b	t	e
v	y	r	s	d	o	r	r	e	a
b	r	p	l	o	b	i	i	e	c
c	l	o	t	h	n	n	c	t	h
w	i	n	g	s	c	g	k	h	w

Complete each sentence with a word from the box.

10. On Saturdays, we like go to the city and _____ people walk by.

11. We put our dog on a _____ and take her with us.

12. Sometimes we _____ for treasures at sidewalk tag sales.

13. At a tag sale, people sell _____ that they don't want any longer.

14. Today, I found a red toy _____ with big black wheels.

15. I saw a hat with a _____ of old silk flowers on it.

16. I'm glad I had some money _____ me!

AT HOME

Ask your child to make a list of things your family might sell at a tag sale and to circle all the words with consonant digraphs.

chair   **ch**ef   **ch**orus

Use a word from the box to name each picture. Write the word. Then circle the sound that the ch in each word stands for.

> **RULE** The consonant digraph **ch** can stand for three different sounds. **ch**air   **ch**ef   **ch**orus

anchor		
chandelier		
chauffeur		
chemist		
chimney		
orchid		

1  ch / sh / k

_____

2 ch / sh / k

_____

3 ch / sh / k

_____

4  ch / sh / k

_____

5  ch / sh / k

_____

6 ch / sh / k

_____

Read the passage. Complete the sentences with words from the box.

anchors
brochure
character
chemistry
Chicago
chief
Michigan
orchestra

Mom brought home a _____ about _____, Illinois. It is the third largest city in the United States and a _____ transportation center on the shores of Lake _____. Huge ships drop their _____ at docks south of the city.

Chicago is an important center of culture as well. Some of the best musicians in the world play in the city's _____. The University of Chicago has world-famous physics and _____ labs there. The city's tall buildings are an important part of its _____.

Name _____

phone

laugh

Read the clues. Use words from the box to complete the puzzle.

| alphabet | autograph | cough | dolphin | elephants |
| laughed | pharaoh | phone | photographs | rough |

Across

2. It's also called the ABCs.

6. This mammal lives in the ocean.

7. This word describes sandpaper.

8. This is an ancient Egyptian ruler.

Down

1. These mammals have long trunks.

2. A famous person might give you this.

3. You need a camera to take these.

4. It's a sign of a cold or a sore throat.

5. Alexander Graham Bell invented this.

Complete each sentence with a word from the box above.

1. We saw a _____ show at the city aquarium.

2. I touched a starfish, and it felt _____.

3. We brought a camera, so we took _____ of the seals.

4. We learned that some whales are much bigger than _____.

5. We _____ when we saw the seals clap for food.

6. When I got home, I ran to the _____ to tell my friend!

AT HOME

Ask your child to choose two words from the puzzle and use them in a sentence.

© Steck-Vaughn Company

shrub   **three**   **school**

RULE A consonant digraph can blend with another consonant to make a three-letter blend.

Unscramble the letters to make a word that names the picture. Write the word.

1 rottah

_____

2 loshoc

_____

3 phrims

_____

4 knirsh

_____

5 darteh

_____

6 cleedush

_____

Read the paragraph. Complete the sentences with words from the box.

Monday was an unlucky day for my family! First, the girl who

delivers the newspaper threw it under the _____. Then

the dog found it and tore it to _____. There was so much

snow that _____ was canceled. My brother Jason had a

sore _____. Mom called the doctor, but the doctor's

_____ was filled all morning. He couldn't see Jason until

_____ o'clock that afternoon. Mom was not exactly

_____ to drive on the slick city streets. But the worst was

yet to come. When we got home, Mom _____. The dog had

eaten the bag of _____ Mom had been thawing for dinner!

| schedule |
| school |
| shreds |
| shrieked |
| shrimp |
| shrubs |
| three |
| thrilled |
| throat |

Name _____

Read the passage. Complete the sentences with words from the box.

My class at _____ is making a scrapbook about

our city. We each took a _____ of a place in the

city. Our _____ took us through the city on the subway.

I took a snapshot of Symphony Hall where the famous city

_____ plays. At the zoo, Anna snapped a picture of a

_____ swinging on a rope. Stephen chose to take a picture of a ship

at the _____. Stephanie took a picture of a _____ at

the aquarium. Phillip took pictures of at least _____ city buses.

Next, we will write about each picture and _____ our scrapbook.

Read each word in the box and listen for the number of syllables you hear. Write each word under the correct heading.

One Syllable	Two Syllables	Three Syllables
_____	_____	_____
_____	_____	_____
_____	_____	_____

AT HOME

Ask your child to write a paragraph about a favorite part of your community and then identify all the words with two syllables.

Read the clues. Use words from the box to complete the puzzle. Then read down the squares to answer the question below.

| camera | chauffeur | dolphin | insect | jungle | knot | orchid | rough |
| schedule | shelf | straw | sugar | throne | traffic | twelve | wrench |

1. a sea mammal

2. It takes snapshots.

3. 10 + 2

4. a place for books

5. a driver

6. something sweet

7. You sip through it.

8. a rain forest

9. a timetable

10. a royal seat

11. a flower

12. not smooth

13. a bug

14. moving cars and trucks

15. You tie this.

16. a plumber's tool

What are the two largest cities in Texas?

_____

Name _____

Unit 2: Spelling Words with Variant Consonants, Consonant Blends,
Silent Letters, and Consonant Digraphs

Use the code to write each missing word.

1 = a	2 = b	3 = c	4 = d	5 = e	6 = f	7 = g	8 = h	9 = i	10 = k
11 = l	12 = n	13 = o	14 = p	15 = r	16 = s	17 = t	18 = u	19 = w	20 = z

1. Cheryl and Brandon know a ___ ___ ___ ___ ___ ___ ___
   16 14 5 3 9 1 11

   ___ ___ ___ ___ ___ in the city.
   14 11 1 3 5

2. Near the playground, there is a rock ___ ___ ___ ___ ___
   11 5 4 7 5

   that looks like a ___ ___ ___ ___ ___ .
   16 17 1 7 5

3. It is far away from the busy ___ ___ ___ ___ ___ ___ ___ and
   17 15 1 6 6 9 3

   the ___ ___ ___ ___ ___ ___ lights.
   2 15 9 7 8 17

4. Cheryl ___ ___ ___ ___ ___ ___ they should ___ ___ ___ ___ ___ ___ ___ ___
   17 8 9 12 10 16   3 8 1 11 11 5 12 7 5

   their friends to enter a talent show.

5. Brandon makes a ___ ___ ___ ___ of people he ___ ___ ___ ___ ___
   11 9 16 17   10 12 13 19 16

   who will want to come.

6. They ___ ___ ___ many ___ ___ ___ ___ ___ ___ to come
   1 16 10   7 18 5 16 17 16

   and watch the show.

7. Anna ___ ___ ___ ___ ___ ___ a ___ ___ ___ ___ on the end of a long pole.
   17 19 9 15 11 16   6 11 1 7

8. Ramon plays a ___ ___ ___ ___ ___ ___ and sings.
   7 18 9 17 1 15

9. Everyone gets a ___ ___ ___ ___ ___ ___ to do their ___ ___ ___ ___ .
   3 8 1 12 3 5   2 5 16 17

10. Everyone wins a ___ ___ ___ ___ ___ , and they all get their
    14 15 9 20 5

    ___ ___ ___ ___ ___ ___ ___ ___ ___ in the newspaper.
    14 8 13 17 13 7 15 1 14 8

Unit 2: Variant Consonants,
Consonant Blends, and Consonant
Digraphs Review

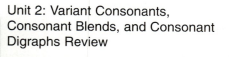

AT HOME

Have your child use the code to write more words that tell what Cheryl and Brandon's friends did in the talent show.

Read the passage. Write complete sentences to answer the questions below.

PHONICS and READING

City Skyscrapers

In 1871, one third of the city of Chicago was destroyed by a huge fire. Architects rushed to Chicago to help rebuild the city. They were looking for a way to house many families and businesses. The architects thought, "Why not build up instead of across? Why not design buildings whose tops would scrape the sky? We could save space on the ground." They began drawing sketches for skyscrapers.

The first skyscraper was only eight stories high when it was built in 1883. A skyscraper with a frame of steel was built in 1890. This skyscraper had nine stories and was about 120 feet high.

In the next one hundred years, skyscrapers began popping up in large cities all over the world. Today tall buildings scrape the sky from New York City to Tokyo.

New York's Empire State Building, which is 1,250 feet high, was once the tallest building in the world. It is no longer the world's tallest building, however. The spires on the Petronas Twin Towers, built in Malaysia in 1996, are 1,758 feet high!

Petronas Twin Towers, Malaysia

1. Where were the first skyscrapers built?

_____

2. Why did the architects design skyscrapers?

_____

3. How tall was the first skyscraper?

_____

4. Where is the tallest building in the world?

_____

5. What is the name of the world's tallest building?

_____

Name _____

Imagine you are an architect. Design a city building for this blank space. Draw a picture of the building and describe it on the lines below. Tell how it would be different from other buildings. The words in the box may help you.

PHONICS and WRITING

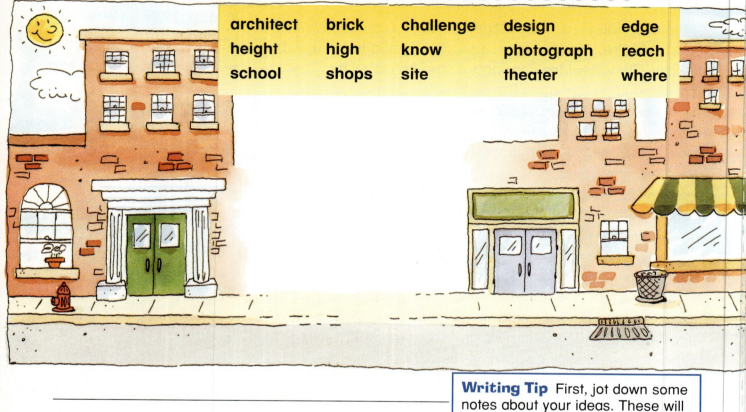

architect	brick	challenge	design	edge
height	high	know	photograph	reach
school	shops	site	theater	where

Writing Tip First, jot down some notes about your ideas. These will help you organize your writing.

_____

_____

_____

_____

_____

_____

_____

_____

_____

_____

AT HOME

Ask your child to read the description to you.

Circle the word that best completes each sentence. Write the word.

1. Josh and I are making a film about _____ in our city who do nice things for other people.

   chauffeur   children

2. Josh's father is letting us use his video _____.

   camera   celery

3. We walk around our city _____ looking for helpful children.

   stretch   streets

4. We see _____ children picking up trash in the park.

   through   three

5. Some third graders from our school are selling _____ cookies for a charity.

   surely   sugar

6. Some Girl Scouts are _____ cars in the school parking lot.

   washing   wringing

7. Then we turn a _____, and we don't know for sure where we are.

   course   corner

8. We find a friendly police officer who says we took a _____ turn.

   rung   wrong

9. She tells us the _____ way to get back to our street.

   right   bright

10. On our way back home, we both _____ down to pick up some litter.

    wish   reach

11. We _____ it into a nearby trash can.

    throw   trunk

12. A little boy rolls by on in-line _____.

    scare   skates

13. He takes a _____ fall right in front of us!

    rough   route

14. We help him up and make _____ he isn't hurt.

    sugar   sure

15. We _____ when we realize that we are being helpful, too!

    cough   laugh

Name _____

Unit 2
CHECK-UP

Say each picture name. Fill in the circle next to the letter or letters that complete each picture name.

1 para___ute
- ○ sh
- ○ ch
- ○ th

2 ___orus
- ○ sh
- ○ ck
- ○ ch

3 ___itar
- ○ g
- ○ gu
- ○ gh

4 ___ins
- ○ tr
- ○ tw
- ○ th

5 ___eese
- ○ sh
- ○ ch
- ○ c

6 ___ity
- ○ c
- ○ s
- ○ ch

7 ___erbil
- ○ g
- ○ j
- ○ c

8 ___ider
- ○ sp
- ○ sh
- ○ sk

9 ___ag
- ○ gl
- ○ fl
- ○ fr

10 pla___
- ○ nt
- ○ ck
- ○ sk

11 ___ale
- ○ th
- ○ wh
- ○ w

12 ___ugar
- ○ s
- ○ sh
- ○ ss

13 ___ool
- ○ sch
- ○ sh
- ○ sc

14 ___ing
- ○ sh
- ○ sw
- ○ str

15 ___orn
- ○ wh
- ○ th
- ○ t

UNIT 3
The Great Outdoors

Irregular Vowel Digraphs, r-Controlled Vowels, Diphthongs

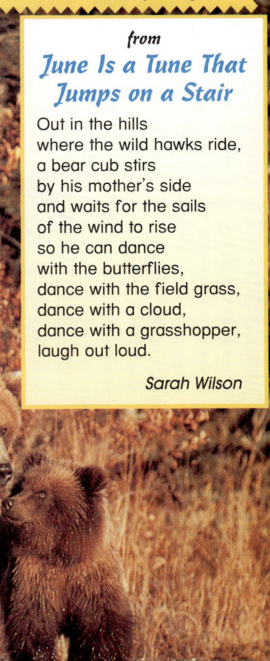

from

June Is a Tune That Jumps on a Stair

Out in the hills
where the wild hawks ride,
a bear cub stirs
by his mother's side
and waits for the sails
of the wind to rise
so he can dance
with the butterflies,
dance with the field grass,
dance with a cloud,
dance with a grasshopper,
laugh out loud.

Sarah Wilson

Think About It

What will the bear cub do when the wind blows?
What in the great outdoors makes you laugh out loud?

Dear Family of _____,

In this unit your child will be learning about *r*-controlled vowels, such as *worm* and *nurse*, diphthongs such as *owl* and *scout*, and vowel digraphs such as *break* and *piece*. Your child will be using these skills to read about the theme of The Great Outdoors. Here are some activities you can do together.

- Write the diphthongs *oy*, *oi*, *ow*, and *ou* on four separate cards, one letter pair per card. Place the cards in an empty box. Take turns drawing a card. Each person must think of a word that has the sound shown on the card, such as *voyage*, *moist*, *crowd*, and *youth*.

- Brainstorm a list of words that contain the vowel digraphs *ie*, *au*, *aw*, and *al*. Think of at least two words for each pair of letters, as in *hawk* and *lawn* or *niece* and *field*. Take turns making up sentences using the pair of words, such as *I saw a hawk on the lawn*.

- Take a walk outdoors with your child and look for things whose names have *r*-controlled vowels, such as *thorns*, *dirt*, *park*, *chair*, or *deer*. Have your child write the words on a nature chart.

LIBRARY LINK

You might like to visit the library and find the book *The Outside Inn* by George Ella Lyon. Read it with your child.

Estimada familia de _____,

En esta unidad, su niño o niña aprenderá los sonidos en inglés de las vocales que vienen antes de la letra *r*, como en *worm* y *nurse*; diptongos como en *owl* y *scout*; además de vocales juntas que tienen un solo sonido, como en *break* y *piece*. Su niño o niña usará estos conocimientos en su lectura sobre Vida al aire libre. Algunas actividades que usted y su niño o niña pueden hacer en inglés aparecen a continuación.

- Escriba los diptongos *oy*, *oi*, *ow* y *ou*, cada uno en una tarjeta. Ponga las tarjetas en una caja vacía. Luego, saque cada uno una tarjeta. Cada persona debe pensar en una palabra que tenga el sonido de las letras que aparecen en la tarjeta, como en *voyage*, *moist*, *crowd*, y *youth*.

- Juntos compongan una lista de palabras con vocales juntas que tengan un solo sonido, como *ie*, *au*, *aw* y *al*. Usen por lo menos dos palabras por cada par de letras, como *hawk* y *lawn* o *niece* y *field*. Túrnense construyendo oraciones que usen el par de palabras, como *I saw a hawk on the lawn*.

- Haga un paseo al aire libre con su niño o niña y busquen objetos cuyos nombres contengan el sonido de una vocal antes de la letra *r*, como en *thorns*, *dirt*, *park*, *chair* o *deer*. Pídale a su niño o niña que escriba las palabras en una gráfica de naturaleza.

bread

piece

Circle the picture name. Write it on the line.

1
sweater
sweeter
swell
_____

2
shark
shriek
shred
_____

3
held
hard
head
_____

4
speed
spread
sprawl
_____

5
feather
father
farther
_____

6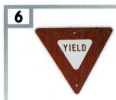
yelled
yawned
yield
_____

7
sealed
shelled
shield
_____

8
throw
thread
three
_____

9
field
feels
filed
_____

Complete each sentence with a word from the box.

10. A hike is a very _____ way to spend the day.

11. The _____ can be a problem, though.

12. Hikers must be _____ for sun, rain, or even snow!

13. It might be so cold out that you can see your _____.

14. Let's walk though this _____ toward the woods.

15. Can you _____ how colorful the fall leaves are?

believe
breath
field
healthy
ready
weather

Name _____

The words in the box are hidden in the puzzle. Circle each word you find. Words can go across or down. Then write each word in the correct column below.

believe	brief	chief	feather	field	health	instead
ready	relief	retrieve	shield	sweater	thread	weather

Short e

_____

_____

_____

_____

_____

_____

_____

Long e

_____

_____

_____

_____

_____

_____

_____

```
r  e  t  r  i  e  v  e  b  y
e  b  h  r  n  h  j  l  e  s
l  s  r  e  s  d  m  r  l  w
i  f  e  a  t  h  e  r  i  e
e  c  a  d  e  e  g  h  e  a
f  h  d  y  a  a  h  t  v  t
f  i  e  l  d  l  r  s  e  e
b  e  w  e  a  t  h  e  r  r
j  f  d  e  s  h  i  e  l  d
z  i  e  c  p  b  r  i  e  f
```

Complete each sentence with a word from the box.

bread	brief	head	pieces	relief	spread

1. Heather and I like to _____ to the park for a picnic.

2. We pack a basket with cheese and freshly baked _____.

3. Heather adds two _____ of cherry pie for dessert.

4. We _____ a blanket under some big oak trees.

5. What a _____ it is to sit down and eat!

6. After we're finished, we take a _____ rest in the shade.

AT HOME

Ask your child to choose two words from the puzzle and use them in a sentence.

book

moon

Use a word from the box to name each picture.
Write the word on the line.

| balloon | football | kangaroo | school | spoon | stool | wood | zoo |

1 _____

2 _____

3 _____

4 _____

5 _____

6 _____

7 _____

8 _____

Follow the directions to write a new word on each line. Then circle each word that has the **oo** sound heard in **book**.

9. Change the first letter in **hook** to **b**. _____

10. Change the first letter to **c**. _____

11. Change the last letter to **p**. _____

12. Change the last letter to **l**. _____

13. Change the first letter to **p**. _____

14. Change the first letter to **w**. _____

15. Change the first letter to **t**. _____

16. Switch the first and last letters. _____

17. Change the first letter to **b**. _____

18. Change the first letter to **f**. _____

Name _____

Use a word from the box to answer each question. Write the word on the line.

boots	brook	broom	cook	crooked	foolish
foot	goose	hood	hook	lookout	moon
noon	notebook	pool	school	snooze	wood

1. Where might a swim team practice? _____

2. Which word describes someone who is acting silly? _____

3. What might you wear on your feet in the rain? _____

4. What person keeps watch for something? _____

5. What big bird makes a honking sound? _____

6. Where do you go to learn to read and write? _____

7. What do you put on the end of a fishing line? _____

8. Which word is another name for *midday*? _____

9. Which word is another name for *stream*? _____

10. What is one way to prepare food? _____

11. What part of your body is attached to your toes? _____

12. Which word is another name for *nap*? _____

13. What do you use to sweep the floor? _____

14. What is attached to a jacket to cover your head? _____

15. Where might you write your homework? _____

16. What appears in the sky nearly every night? _____

17. What building material do we get from trees? _____

18. Which word means "not straight"? _____

AT HOME

Have your child read the words and tell which have the vowel sound heard in **book** and which have the vowel sound heard in **moon**.

© Steck-Vaughn Company

haul   **paw**   **chalk**

Write the letters to complete each word.

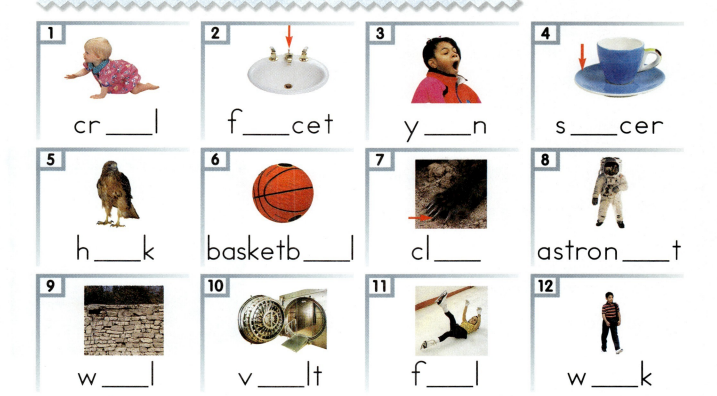

1. cr____l

2. f____cet

3. y____n

4. s____cer

5. h____k

6. basketb____l

7. cl____

8. astron____t

9. w____l

10. v____lt

11. f____l

12. w____k

Read each sentence. Circle each word that has the vowel digraph au, aw, or al. Then write the words below.

13. My favorite season is autumn, when the weather is cool but not raw.

14. We can have fun as we talk and draw on the sidewalk.

15. I got a small wallet for my birthday in August.

16. Add salt to the sauce, but don't scald it.

17. Don't put the laundry in the sink with the leaky faucet.

18. Beware of the cat's claws when you take the thorn from its paw.

_____ _____ _____ _____ _____

_____ _____ _____ _____ _____

_____ _____ _____ _____ _____

Name _____

Complete each sentence with a word from the box.

almost	also
always	audience
author	awe
caught	dawn
drawings	recall
smallest	talk

1. Nature has _____ inspired artists.

2. When you visit an art museum, _____ with your friends about paintings of nature.

3. Observe the _____ details by looking closely at colors, shapes, and patterns.

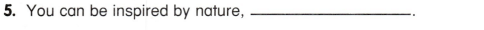

4. Did the artists look at the outdoors with wonder and _____?

5. You can be inspired by nature, _____.

6. Find a special spot that you can visit _____ every week.

7. Be the _____ of your very own nature journal.

8. Record what you observe at different times, such as _____ and dusk.

9. Make _____ with pencils or crayons to go with your writing.

10. Scenes _____ on film can be wonderful, too.

11. Find a way to share your work with an _____.

12. Show your artwork or share a moment you _____ from your past.

AT HOME

Have your child tell whether the vowel digraph in each word from the box comes at the beginning, middle, or end of the word.

sle**igh**   **th**ey

Draw a line to match each word with its clue.

Words	Clues
1. eight	what you say to get someone's attention
2. prey	people who live near you
3. veil	a large, horse-drawn sled
4. sleigh	to follow orders
5. they	used to control a horse
6. freight	more than one person or thing
7. obey	5 + 3
8. neighbors	a cloth that covers a person's face
9. vein	to find out how heavy an object is
10. weigh	goods carried over land, air, or water
11. hey	something that is hunted
12. reins	a tube that carries blood through the body

Complete each sentence with a word from above.

13. My sister and I like to watch hawks and other birds of _____ flying.

14. These birds are so graceful as _____ soar across the sky.

15. We saw seven or _____ bald eagles fly above the mountains.

16. You must train a horse to _____ your commands.

17. Use the _____ to make the horse go where you want.

18. A _____ is one way to travel over frozen country roads.

Name _____

scr**ew**   **fr**u**it**

Choose a word from the box to name each picture. Write the word on the line.

1

jewel	crew
dew	mew

_____

_____

_____

2

juice	fruit
cruise	suit

_____

_____

_____

Complete each sentence with a word from the box.

blew   brewing   dew   few   flew   fruit   grew   knew   nephew   threw

3. Uncle Paul went camping with his _____ Matt.

4. They ate some _____ after they put up the tent.

5. Suddenly, they saw that a storm was _____.

6. Uncle Paul _____ that they had to get ready for the storm.

7. They _____ all the loose gear into the truck.

8. They began to hear a _____ raindrops.

9. Then the wind _____ and the rain poured.

10. The storm _____ louder, and later it became quiet again.

11. The next morning, the _____ sparkled on the ground.

12. It was as if the storm _____ right over us like a bird.

AT HOME

Ask your child to read the sentences to you. Then choose several words from the word box and ask your child to spell them.

© Steck-Vaughn Company

Make rhyming word pairs to answer each riddle. Choose words from the box that have the same vowel digraph as the word in dark letters. The first one is done for you.

all	brief
chalk	crew
fault	fruit
instead	loose
nook	weather
weight	yawn

1. What do you call it when it is raining **feathers**?

    <u>feather</u>   <u>weather</u>

2. What do you call a boring time in your front **lawn**?

    _____ _____

3. What do you call a **ball** game that everyone can play?

    _____ _____

4. What do you call a **goose** that has gotten out of its pen?

    _____ _____

5. What do you call a mistake made while trying to pole **vault**?

    _____ _____

6. What do you call a small place where a **crook** hides?

    _____ _____

7. What do you call a person who was **chief** for a short time?

    _____ _____

8. What do you call a **talk** your teacher makes at the board?

    _____ _____

9. What do you call the heaviness of a **freight** shipment?

    _____ _____

10. What do you call **stew** made for a group of workers?

    _____ _____

11. What do you call a choice of **bread** rather than crackers?

    _____ _____

12. What do you call a **suit** that is made of apples and pears?

    _____ _____

Name _____

Read each word in the box and listen for the number of syllables. Then write each word in the correct column. Circle the vowel digraph (**ea, ie, oo, au, aw, al, ei, ey, ui,** or **ew**) in each word.

alternate	altogether	autograph	automatic
awkward	briefly	cautionary	cruise
fault	fool	misunderstood	neighborhood
obey	pleasant	shriek	steadily

One Syllable   **Two Syllables**   **Three Syllables**   **Four Syllables**

_____   _____   _____   _____

_____   _____   _____   _____

_____   _____   _____   _____

_____   _____   _____   _____

Read each sentence below. Circle the words with three syllables.

1. My scout troop is planning a dinosaur hunt.

2. It is really an alternate to a hunt, because dinosaurs are extinct.

3. We will search for authentic fossils.

4. Such fossils have already been found in our city.

5. It would be awfully interesting to find something from so long ago.

6. Maybe the newspapers would be interested in the story.

AT HOME

Read a newspaper article with your child. Have your child point out and read words with three or more syllables.

Read the article. Then answer the questions below.

Sidewalk Fun

Just because you live in a city doesn't mean you can't have fun outdoors. You don't need a field or a lawn. A sidewalk is a great outdoor place. Here are a few ideas for city sidewalk fun. You can do almost all of these things by yourself or with a group of friends.

Before beginning, check your neighborhood's rules and obey them. For example, some places don't permit roller-skating or bike riding on the sidewalk. However, you can play hopscotch or handball. You can jump rope. You can draw a beautiful scene on the sidewalk with colored chalk.

In warm weather, you can brew sun tea. Fill a large jar with cool water. Drop in four tea bags and screw on the lid. Let the jar sit in the sun for a few hours. The water will slowly become tea. Pour the tea over ice for a good drink.

Have a planting party. Spread out pots, seeds, sprouts, soil, and tools on the sidewalk. Explain to neighbors how to fill pots with soil. Show them how to plant seeds or sprouts and add water. Care for the plants for a few weeks. Then share the flowers, vegetables, or herbs you grew with people at a shelter or food bank. They will appreciate it.

1. What should you do before beginning a sidewalk activity?

   _____

2. What are some sidewalk activities that most neighborhoods will allow?

   _____

3. How can you make tea without boiling water?

   _____

4. What does the article suggest doing with the plants you grow?

   _____

Name _____

What is your favorite way to have fun outdoors? Write a paragraph about it. The words in the box may help you.

PHONICS and WRITING

ball	balloon	brook	crew	draw
health	lawn	look	neighbor	notebook
piece	they	tool	walk	weather

_____

_____

> **WRITING TIP** It is important to get your ideas down on paper quickly.

_____

_____

_____

_____

_____

_____

_____

_____

AT HOME

Ask your child to read the paragraph to you.

car

corn

Write the letters to complete each word that has the ar sound.

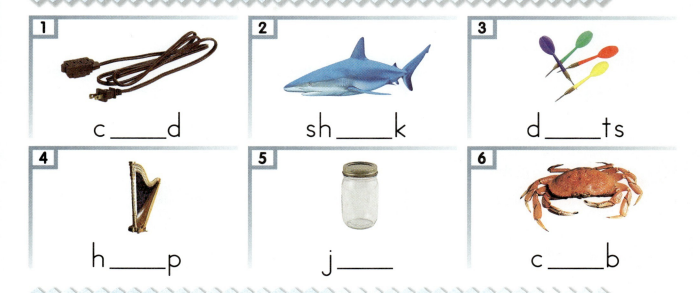

1. c____d

2. sh____k

3. d____ts

4. h____p

5. j____

6. c____b

Write the letters to complete each word that has the or sound.

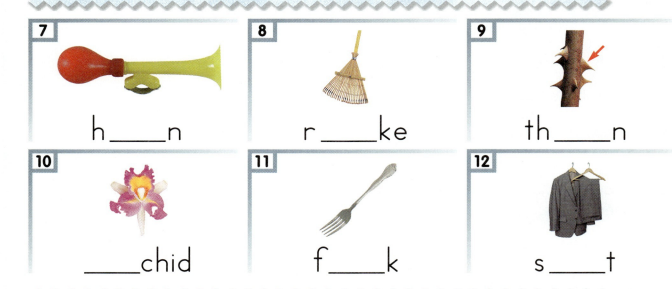

7. h____n

8. r____ke

9. th____n

10. ____chid

11. f____k

12. s____t

Draw lines to match pairs of words with the same vowel sounds.

13. garden   porch

14. story   barn

15. market   park

16. morning   store

17. harm   born

18. forty   alarm

Name _____

worm   **bird**   **nurse**   **fern**

RULE The letters **or, ir, ur,** and **er** can all stand for the same vowel sound. You can hear that vowel sound in w**or**m, b**ir**d, n**ur**se, and f**er**n.

Circle the picture name. Write it on the line.

1

sheet
stork
shield
shirt

_____

2

hammer
head
heart
helmet

_____

3

ruler
razor
reader
roast

_____

4

gerbil
guitar
gym
giraffe

_____

5
13
thread
twelve
thirteen
thrill

_____

6

tiger
triangle
turn
turtle

_____

Complete each sentence with a word from the box.

7. What kind of wildlife is right _____ your feet?

8. You might be _____ by what you can find.

9. Perhaps you'll watch a bird fly from its _____ high in a tree.

10. You can see _____ run along the ground gathering nuts.

11. Underground you'll find a whole new _____.

12. Dig carefully into the grass and _____.

13. You'll find more than just _____ inching around.

14. _____ have told us that many tiny animals live underground.

15. Let us know if they _____ right!

dirt
experts
perch
squirrels
surprised
under
were
world
worms

AT HOME

Ask your child to make up new sentences using words from the word box.

square　　　**chair**　　　**bear**

RULE The letters **are, air,** and **ear** can stand for the vowel sound heard in squ**are**, ch**air**, and b**ear**.

Complete each sentence with a word from the box.

1. When you visit the great outdoors,

be _____ of wild animals.

2. _____ live in many national parks.

3. You may see them as they _____ for winter.

4. These large mammals eat meat and fruit,

such as _____ and apples.

5. Bears can smell the _____ and sense humans.

6. They can rise up and stand on a sturdy _____ of hind legs.

7. If you see the _____ of a bear, simply walk away.

8. Do not run, because your movement might _____ the bear.

9. Don't ever _____ a bear to catch you.

10. Bears have a _____ for running and can travel 25 miles per hour.

11. An angry bear can use its sharp claws to _____ at its enemy.

12. You should never disturb the _____ of a mother bear and her cubs.

13. In the past, hunters have not _____ the lives of wild bears.

14. Sightings of grizzly bears have become very _____.

15. People just need to take _____ when they visit bear country.

air
aware
bears
care
dare
flair
lair
pair
pears
prepare
rare
scare
spared
stare
tear

Name _____

beard

cheer

Earth

**Circle the word that completes each sentence.
Write the word on the line.**

1. If you could _____ into the future, what job would you like to have?

peer
tear
pair

2. Is a _____ in wildlife management for you?

fear
career
sneer

3. To find out more, visit a wildlife area _____ you.

dear
bear
near

4. It is never too _____ to ask questions.

early
nearly
yearly

5. Talk to someone who can _____ you toward information.

steer
hear
clear

6. Find out where that person studied to _____ about wildlife management.

pearl
rear
learn

7. Ask what a wildlife manager does in each season of the _____.

smear
year
yard

8. Getting such a job takes more than _____ luck.

sheer
hear
near

9. It is _____ that we will need wildlife managers in the future.

dear
steer
clear

10. It takes plenty of hard work to keep _____ healthy.

Worth
Earth
Birth

AT HOME

Help your child make up a cheer for Earth using words with the vowel sounds heard in ***beard, cheer,*** and ***Earth.***

© Steck-Vaughn Company

Complete each sentence with a word from the box.

air	better	care	cheers	coral
dirt	Earth	explore	heard	hurting
learn	park	water	world	year

1. Try to leave the outdoors in _____ shape than you found it.

2. Everything we do has an effect on our planet, _____.

3. We can _____ to take care of our home.

4. We breathe the _____.

5. We drink the _____.

6. Much of our food grows from seeds planted in the _____.

7. We should keep this in mind as we _____ our world.

8. After a picnic in the _____, pick up all the trash.

9. It is all right to snorkel in a _____ reef, but don't harm the creatures there.

10. Every place in the _____ needs our help.

11. We can all try to take _____ of our planet.

12. We should work to help Earth every day of the _____.

13. What would you do if you _____ that your friends were littering?

14. Would you tell them that they were _____ Earth?

15. If so, you earn three _____!

Name _____

Complete each sentence with a word from the box. Then write the number of syllables in the word.

atmosphere	bark	bear	certainly	consider
evergreen	forests	furniture	important	major
numerous	serve	surrounding	urban	yards

1. Planting a tree is one of the most _____ ways ____ to help our planet.

2. Trees help people and animals in _____ ways. ____

3. Trees improve the air quality by adding oxygen to

   the _____. ____

4. Trees play a _____ role by keeping soil from eroding. ____

5. In national _____, trees provide habitats for animals. ____

6. Even dead trees _____ this function. ____

7. As dead trees rot, they add nutrients to

   the _____ soil. ____

8. Trees that _____ fruit provide a source for healthy food. ____

9. Tree _____ is used to make medicine and other products. ____

10. Tables, chairs, desks, and other _____ are made of wood from trees. ____

11. Please _____ planting a tree. ____

12. It is _____ one of the best ways to help Earth. ____

13. Plant an oak, an _____, or a fruit tree soon. ____

Ask your child to find other words that have one, two, or three syllables in the sentences above.

Find the hidden word in the letters that follow each sentence. Write the word on the line. The words in the box will help you.

bear	book	chair	conserve	drew
first	launch	lawn	neighbor	piece
pool	prey	urban	walk	weather

1. It's a predator's target.   t r p r h e w y   _____

2. This large mammal is fond of honey.   b e i a r   _____

3. This word describes a city.   p u r c f g b a n   _____

4. This word means "to be careful
   with resources."   b c o y n s e m b r v e   _____

5. This person lives near you.   r n c h e i p g h p b o e r   _____

6. This is one part of something.   b p i e n u c e   _____

7. Have a seat on this.   p c h e a t i r w   _____

8. This is the opposite of *last*.   s h f i r e s t a   _____

9. This word rhymes with *crew*.   d r m l e a w s   _____

10. This is another word for *grass*.   o l p a w a r n   _____

11. You do this when you travel on foot.   w j s a e a l k   _____

12. This word rhymes with *feather*.   w o p e a r t h a t e r   _____

13. This word means "to send off."   l u n a u n c h   _____

14. This is something to read.   b e a k o o p k   _____

15. This is a place to swim.   p o l e o l e   _____

Name _____

Draw lines to connect the words that have the same vowel sound as the word in dark letters. Trace a path on the cloud, on the tree trunk, and in the stream. Begin with the underlined words.

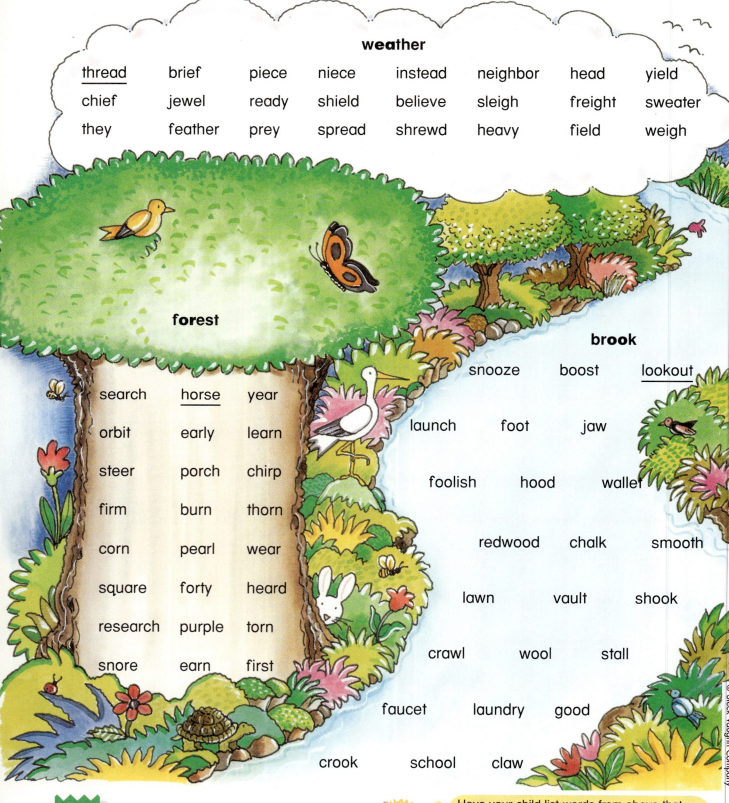

weather

thread	brief	piece	niece	instead	neighbor	head	yield
chief	jewel	ready	shield	believe	sleigh	freight	sweater
they	feather	prey	spread	shrewd	heavy	field	weigh

forest

search	horse	year
orbit	early	learn
steer	porch	chirp
firm	burn	thorn
corn	pearl	wear
square	forty	heard
research	purple	torn
snore	earn	first

brook

snooze	boost	lookout
launch	foot	jaw
foolish	hood	wallet
redwood	chalk	smooth
lawn	vault	shook
crawl	wool	stall
faucet	laundry	good
crook	school	claw

AT HOME

Have your child list words from above that have the same vowel sounds.

© Steck-Vaughn Company

boy

coins

Circle the picture name. Write it on the line.

1

boil
bike
boys
_____

2

toils
toys
toss
_____

3
pint
port
point
_____

4

coil
coal
coy
_____

5

oil
ostrich
oyster
_____

6
soil
soul
soy
_____

7
broken
bray
broil
_____

8

foil
follow
foul
_____

9
nose
noise
nice
_____

Match each word from the box to its definition. Write the word.

annoy	destroy	employ	enjoy	moist
poison	royalty	toy	voice	voyage

10. kings and queens _____

11. a little wet _____

12. heard when you speak _____

13. to hire _____

14. a harmful substance _____

15. to ruin _____

16. to make angry _____

17. a trip _____

18. to have a good time _____

19. a plaything _____

Name _____

Complete each sentence with a word from the box.

| annoying | avoid | boy | choice | disappointment | employ |
| enjoy | join | oily | ointments | poison | spoiled |

1. Camping and hiking are pastimes that many people _____.

2. _____ and Girl Scout troops often visit the great outdoors.

3. Friends often _____ each other for weekend camping fun.

4. A camping trip can be _____ by contact with some common plants.

5. Know what plants to _____ as you hike and explore.

6. Become familiar with _____ ivy, oak, and sumac.

7. The leaves of such plants contain an _____ substance that causes a rash.

8. An _____ itch develops from such a rash.

9. Know what methods to _____ if you do touch a poisonous plant.

10. Special creams and _____ can help stop the rash.

11. Don't suffer the _____ of having your trip ruined.

12. Make the right _____ by avoiding poisonous plants.

Poison ivy

Poison oak

Poison sumac

Unit 3: Reading Diphthongs **oy** and **oi** in Context

AT HOME

Ask your child to think of other words that are spelled with **oy** or **oi**.

cow

crow

RULE The letters **ow** can stand for either the vowel sound heard in **cow** or the vowel sound heard in cr**ow**.

Circle the picture name. Write it on the line.

1

ball
book
bowl
_____

2

claw
clown
clock
_____

3
crowd
crawl
crew
_____

4

mew
mow
mole
_____

5
doll
dune
down
_____

6

roof
row
roll
_____

Write the words from the box in the correct columns.

ow as in cow

_____
_____
_____
_____
_____
_____
_____
_____

ow as in crow

_____
_____
_____
_____
_____
_____
_____
_____

allow	arrow
below	brown
crown	eyebrow
flower	follow
glow	gown
owl	pillow
plow	slow
snow	tomorrow

Name _____

soup   **cough**   **couple**   **four**   **mouse**

Circle the word that completes each sentence.
Write the word on the line.

1. Our _____ group is planning a trip.

youth
your
you

2. We are going to hike high in the _____.

mound
moth
mountains

3. Our group will camp near the _____ of a river.

mouth
mow
moist

4. I hope that we have _____ time to hike and fish.

employ
ear
enough

5. We plan to catch lots of _____ and other fish.

trough
trout
tough

6. We will take photos of the beautiful _____.

countryside
clowns
corduroy

7. We will _____ around for interesting animals to watch.

soup
scout
snow

8. I have _____ about this camping trip for weeks.

tear
thought
thorn

9. We have _____ all our supplies.

bought
bowl
blouse

10. I am ready for an _____ adventure!

owl
outdoor
oyster

Have your child find and list words with the five sounds for **ou**.

Read each word. Write the number of vowels you see in the word, the number of vowels you hear, and the number of syllables the word has.

	Vowels		
	Seen	Heard	Syllables
resourceful	_____	_____	_____
downtown	_____	_____	_____
boyhood	_____	_____	_____
fourteen	_____	_____	_____
windowsill	_____	_____	_____
poisonous	_____	_____	_____
snowbound	_____	_____	_____
throughout	_____	_____	_____
corduroy	_____	_____	_____
eyebrow	_____	_____	_____

	Vowels		
	Seen	Heard	Syllables
double	_____	_____	_____
tough	_____	_____	_____
thoughtful	_____	_____	_____
slower	_____	_____	_____
employer	_____	_____	_____
powerful	_____	_____	_____
mountainside	_____	_____	_____
countdown	_____	_____	_____
embroider	_____	_____	_____
royal	_____	_____	_____

Read each sentence. Circle the words with two syllables.

1. Alisha works in her flower beds a couple of days each week.

2. Some of her yellow flowers have sprouted.

3. The flowers must have enough moisture and avoid too much sun.

4. Alisha looks proudly at her flowers and enjoys them.

5. She shares her flowers with a couple of friends around the neighborhood.

Name _____

Complete each sentence with a word from the box.

amount	avoid	caught	choice	double
enough	found	ground	moisten	mound
outdoors	scout	source	through	touch

1. Sometimes when you are camping _____, you can build a fire.

2. Families can make the _____ to build a fire in some parks.

3. _____ around the area for tinder, such as dry leaves or twigs.

4. Kindling is larger than tinder and should be dry _____ to snap.

5. Fuel is larger wood that is at least _____ the size of kindling.

6. Clear a fire circle and make a _____ of tinder in the center.

7. Make a small triangle over the tinder with three pieces of kindling that

   _____ at the top.

8. Ask an adult to strike a match and hold it under

   the tinder at _____ level.

9. When the tinder has _____ fire, add
   more kindling.

10. Then add the _____ of fuel that you need.

11. Take care to conserve fuel to _____ smoke pollution.

12. If you need a heat _____ for cooking, use the coals as the
    fire burns down.

13. When you are _____ with the fire, let it die down until
    only ashes are left.

14. Stir the ashes, _____ them with sprinkles of water,
    and stir again.

15. Return the campsite to the way you _____ it.

AT HOME

Ask your child to read the sentences to you.

PHONICS and SPELLING

In each sentence, the word oyster stands for one of the words in the box. Write the correct words on the lines below.

1. Let's go hiking in the great <u>oyster</u>!
2. <u>Oyster</u> this trail, and we'll learn a lot about nature.
3. We'll make it a <u>oyster</u> to be careful on our hike.
4. We'll always keep the safety of our <u>oyster</u> in mind.
5. No one wants to step on a <u>oyster</u> snake!
6. We don't want to <u>oyster</u> any animals' habitats, either.
7. This <u>oyster</u> region has very steep trails.
8. If we hiked here in winter, we might get <u>oyster</u>.
9. There are lots of natural <u>oyster</u> in these hills.
10. Let's <u>oyster</u> around for some wildlife to observe.
11. I see a field of buttercups and other <u>oyster</u> over there.
12. That bird has a crest that looks like a king's <u>oyster</u>.
13. Listen to the hooting of that horned <u>oyster</u>!
14. I <u>oyster</u> that they only hunted at night.
15. If I slept in the woods, I'd make a <u>oyster</u> of pine needles.
16. I like living in the <u>oyster</u>, not in the city.
17. My <u>oyster</u> has a view of distant, snowy mountains.
18. I will always <u>oyster</u> being in the great outdoors.

coiled	country
crown	destroy
enjoy	flowers
follow	group
mountainous	outdoors
owl	pillow
point	resources
scout	snowbound
thought	window

1. _____ 2. _____ 3. _____

4. _____ 5. _____ 6. _____

7. _____ 8. _____ 9. _____

10. _____ 11. _____ 12. _____

13. _____ 14. _____ 15. _____

16. _____ 17. _____ 18. _____

Name

Read each word. Circle a word in each row that rhymes with the word on the left. At the bottom of the page, write each dark letter to find the answer to the riddle.

1.	cow	how	mow
2.	broil	bowl	coil
3.	trout	shout	treat
4.	tough	enough	trough
5.	mound	source	pound
6.	crow	show	cow
7.	pour	power	four
8.	bound	pound	group
9.	scout	pout	soup
10.	caught	count	taught
11.	coin	join	cloud
12.	annoy	about	enjoy
13.	double	around	trouble
14.	employ	destroy	loud
15.	power	mower	shower
16.	soup	south	group

How do mountains hear?

$\overline{}\ \overline{}\ \overline{}\ \overline{}\quad \overline{}\ \overline{}\ \overline{}\ \overline{}\ \overline{}\ \overline{}\ \overline{}\ \overline{}\ \overline{}\ \overline{}\ \overline{}\ \overline{}$
1 2 3 4   5 6 7 8 9 10 11 12 13 14 15 16

AT HOME

Ask your child to name another rhyming word for each pair of words.

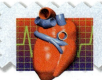

Read the passage. Then answer the questions below.

PHONICS and READING

Theme Hikes

Are you aware that hiking is a healthful exercise? Walking gets your muscles moving and certainly increases your energy. To make your hikes more enjoyable, choose a theme for your outdoor exploration. Here are some ideas for a theme hike.

Mark the Trail. Try this hike with a crowd. Divide your crew into two groups. Have one group start out by outlining a trail with markers, such as crossed branches or piles of stones placed on the ground. Then the second group follows the markers, picking them up as they go.

Story Frame Hike. This is a good hike for a small group of hikers. Every couple of yards, stop and frame a picture with your hands. Share the thoughts that come to mind about the area in your frame.

An Ecosystem Hike. This works best with a large group. As you walk along, point out plants and animals whose survival are linked. Try to list a food chain, such as soil, grass, worm, sparrow, hawk, for the habitats around the trail.

A Silent Hike. This hike works well for a group of any size. Tell all the hikers to make as little sound as possible. Go through the area trying not to make any noise. Listen instead for all the sounds in the woods around you.

Stone marker

1. Why is hiking a healthful exercise?

_____

2. What might you use to mark a trail so that others can follow it?

_____

3. After you have framed a picture on the story frame hike, what should you do?

_____

4. What might you learn on the ecosystem hike?

_____

5. Why should you keep quiet on the silent hike?

_____

Name _____

Create your own theme hike. What is the name of the hike? What will you do on the hike? With what size group does the hike work best? Write a paragraph explaining the hike. The words in the box may help you.

PHONICS and WRITING

around	clear	enjoy
explore	follow	forest
found	group	point
prepare	scout	star
through	turtle	world

_____

_____

_____

_____

_____

_____

_____

_____

_____

_____

_____

WRITING TIP Don't worry about writing a perfect first draft. You will have time to revise your work later.

AT HOME

Have your child read the paragraph to you. Help your child plan a time for your family to participate in the hike.

Circle the word that completes each sentence.
Write the word on the line.

1. An owl hunts for its _____ at night.

   prey
   paw
   pair

2. The explorers took a _____ on the high seas.

   vein
   visor
   voyage

3. We shifted our bikes into first _____ to go uphill.

   gear
   germ
   girth

4. The library is downtown just _____ of the bridge.

   source
   shower
   south

5. Aunt Cathy will visit her nephew and _____ next week.

   knead
   niece
   noose

6. The ground is _____ after the light rain.

   mourn
   mound
   moist

7. Ms. Henley had to _____ our costumes after the play.

   rare
   repair
   rear

8. Wash your hands before you _____ any food.

   touch
   though
   town

9. The Jacksons are our next-door _____.

   neighbors
   nephew
   grooms

10. We are expecting _____ people for the party.

    foil
    forty
    fought

Name _____

Fill in the circle next to the word that completes each sentence.

1. Jamie will watch the stars tonight after _____.
   - ○ doubt
   - ○ dark
   - ○ double
   - ○ draw

2. I've never been to a rain forest, but I'd like to _____ more about them.
   - ○ learn
   - ○ loud
   - ○ loyal
   - ○ loose

3. My mother belongs to a reading _____ that meets once a month.
   - ○ group
   - ○ gear
   - ○ ground
   - ○ gown

4. Uncle Jeff's fishing trip begins in the morning at _____.
   - ○ destroy
   - ○ dawn
   - ○ down
   - ○ drew

5. Tyrone wants to _____ his new shirt tomorrow.
   - ○ wool
   - ○ worse
   - ○ weigh
   - ○ wear

6. Selena spreads peanut butter on the _____.
   - ○ bought
   - ○ bread
   - ○ brief
   - ○ bear

7. Lory's favorite color is _____.
   - ○ purple
   - ○ pear
   - ○ pair
   - ○ prepare

8. Mr. Garcia taught us about how _____ fly south for the winter.
   - ○ books
   - ○ barns
   - ○ birds
   - ○ boys

9. The horse is asleep in its _____.
   - ○ stall
   - ○ stew
   - ○ salt
   - ○ store

10. Let's call home so our family won't _____ about us.
    - ○ weather
    - ○ window
    - ○ wood
    - ○ worry

11. Doug's sister _____ out all the candles on her birthday cake.
    - ○ believe
    - ○ blew
    - ○ brook
    - ○ bow

12. A _____ is growing in a basket on our porch.
    - ○ fern
    - ○ foolish
    - ○ first
    - ○ foil

Long Ago

Syllables and Word Structure

Pachycephalosaurus
(pak-i-sef-a-lo-saw-rus)

Among the later dinosaurs
  Though not the largest, strongest,
PACHYCEPHALOSAURUS had
  The name that was the longest.

Yet he had more than syllables,
  As you may well suppose.
He had great knobs upon his cheeks
  And spikes upon his nose.

Ten inches thick, atop his head,
  A bump of bone projected.
By this his brain, though hardly worth
  Protecting, was protected.

No claw or tooth, no tree that fell
  Upon his head kerwhacky,
Could crack or crease or jar or scar
  That stony part of Paky.

And so he nibbled plants in peace
  And lived untroubled days.
Sometimes, in fact, as Paky proved,
  To be a bonehead pays.

Richard Armour

Think About It

Why does the poet say "though hardly worth protecting"?
Do you think it ever pays to be a "bonehead"?

Dear Family of _____,

Your child will be learning about syllables and word endings. Your child will use these skills to read about the theme of Long Ago. Here are some activities you can do together.

- Ask your child to look around the house for items whose names are compound words, such as *dishcloth* or *newspaper*. Try to find ten compound words. Have your child write half of each compound word on an index card, such as *news* on one card and *paper* on a second card. Play a game of Go Fish. Match the words to form compounds.

- Write ten words on separate index cards and put them in a container. Have your child draw a card and read the word aloud. Then have your child tell you how many syllables are in the word.

- Look at the picture below. Encourage your child to write a story, using as many words as possible that have word endings, such as *ed, ing, er,* and *est.* Here are some words to help your child begin writing the story: *tiniest, bigger, wading, tallest, flying,* or *hopped.*

LIBRARY LINK

You might like to visit the library and find the book *Life Story* by Eric Maddern. Read it with your child.

Estimada familia de _____,

Su niño o niña aprenderá sobre las sílabas y los sufijos de algunas palabras en inglés. Usará estos conocimientos en su lectura sobre Tiempos pasados. Algunas actividades que usted y su niño o niña pueden hacer en inglés aparecen a continuación.

- Pídale a su niño o niña que busque objetos por la casa que tengan nombres compuestos, como *dishcloth* o *newspaper*. Vean si pueden encontrar diez objetos de palabras compuestas. Luego, pídale a su niño o niña que escriba cada una de las palabras que forman la palabra compuesta en una tarjeta, como *news* en una y *paper* en otra. Juntos jueguen a "Go Fish". Emparejen las palabras para formar nuevas palabras compuestas.

- Escriba diez palabras en tarjetas individuales y póngalas en un recipiente. Pídale a su niño o niña que escoja una tarjeta y que lea la palabra en voz alta. Luego, su niño o niña debe decirle el número de sílabas de la palabra.

- Miren el dibujo que aparece arriba. Pídale a su niño o niña que escriba un cuento y que use tantas palabras como pueda que tengan al final *-ed, -ing, -er* y *-est*. A continuación aparecen algunas palabras que ayudarán a su niño o niña a empezar a escribir el cuento: *tiniest, bigger, wading, tallest, flying* o *hopped.*

Read the words below. If the word has more than one syllable, draw a line to divide the word into syllables.

1. corner
2. whole
3. gloom
4. picnic
5. charcoal
6. canvas
7. harvest
8. tractor
9. practice
10. costume

Circle the words in the maze that have two syllables. Draw a line to connect the circled words to show the best route for the student to get to school.

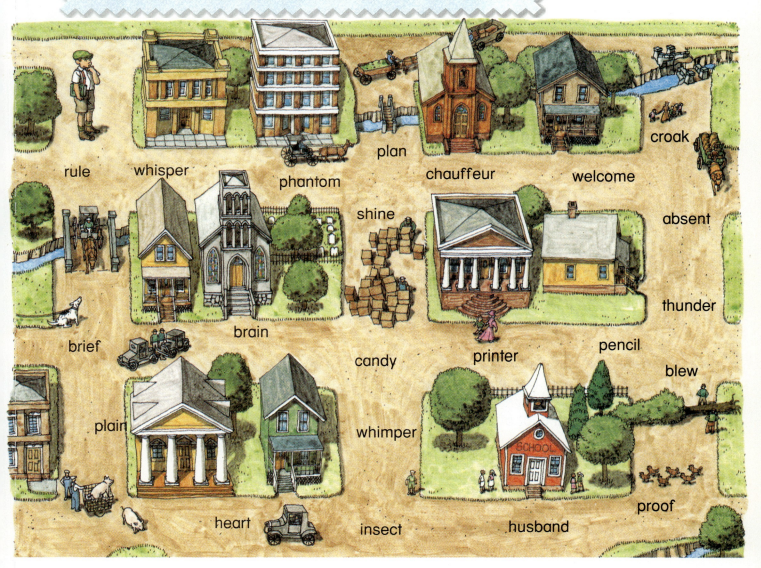

rule   whisper   plan   phantom   chauffeur   welcome   croak

shine   absent

brain   thunder

brief   candy   printer   pencil   blew

plain   whimper

heart   insect   husband   proof

Name _____

Write the words from the box in the correct list below. Then draw a line to divide each word into syllables.

| dragon | famous | menu | paper | pilot |
| rigid | robin | salad | sofa | tiger |

First Vowel Sound Short

_____

_____

_____

_____

_____

First Vowel Sound Long

_____

_____

_____

_____

_____

Draw lines to divide these words into syllables. Then complete each sentence with one of these words.

timid	climate	magic	pupils
women	label	frozen	humid
under	tulips	solid	panic

1. In pioneer times, _____ often made their own clothes.

2. Some people say the _____ has become warmer in the past one hundred years.

3. When the air has a lot of water in it, we say it is _____.

4. It was so cold this winter that the lake was _____ solid.

5. _____ are flowers that come from Holland.

6. My music teacher has many _____.

AT HOME Ask your child to write four more two-syllable words and divide them into syllables.

Read each word. Write the number of vowel sounds you hear. Then write the word and draw lines to divide it into syllables.

	Vowel Sounds	Divided into Syllables		Vowel Sounds	Divided into Syllables
1. over	___	_____	2. create	___	_____
3. pleasant	___	_____	4. reason	___	_____
5. rely	___	_____	6. crouch	___	_____
7. science	___	_____	8. unite	___	_____
9. telephone	___	_____	10. giant	___	_____
11. quiet	___	_____	12. piano	___	_____
13. guitar	___	_____	14. saucer	___	_____

Write these words in the correct list below.

dial	elephant	faucet
idea	quit	realize
seal	thousand	train

One Syllable	Two Syllables	Three Syllables
_____	_____	_____
_____	_____	_____
_____	_____	_____

Name _____

Read the words in the box. Draw lines to divide the words into syllables.

ago	American	another	comics
editor	estimate	favorite	hundred
local	once	pioneers	printed
regularly	sixty	throughout	written

Choose a word from the box to complete each sentence. Write the word. Then write the number of syllables in the word.

1. Long _____ people had a difficult time getting the news. _____

2. In the 1400s, Germans became _____ in the newspaper business. _____

3. In the next two _____ years, newspapers spread throughout Europe. _____

4. The first newspaper in the _____ colonies was published in Boston in 1690. _____

5. This news sheet was only printed _____ and was never seen again. _____

6. In 1704, _____ newspaper was printed in Boston, and then it came out regularly. _____

7. Experts _____ that there are sixty thousand newspapers in the world today. _____

8. Many towns print small newspapers that report _____ news. _____

9. Have you ever _____ a letter to the editor of a newspaper? _____

10. The _____ is in charge of the content of a newspaper. _____

11. What is your _____ section of the newspaper? _____

12. My favorite part is the _____ page. _____

AT HOME

Ask your child to read a newspaper article aloud. Have your child tell how many syllables are in some of the words.

Read the words in the box. Draw lines to divide the words into syllables.

briefcase	earring	fireplace	flashlight
padlock	postmark	seafood	songbird
soundproof	snowshoes	sweatband	toothpaste

Answer each clue with a word from the box above. Then answer the question below by reading the word in the shaded boxes.

1. A working person might carry this.

2. shrimp, for example

3. to shut out sound

4. used on a trunk or locker

5. This has a hearth and a mantle.

6. exercise wear

7. It helps you see in the dark.

8. a piece of jewelry

9. a robin, for example

10. They help you walk in deep snow.

11. Clean your teeth with this.

1. __ __ __ __ ▨ __ __ __
2. __ __ ▨ __ __
3. __ __ __ __ ▨ __ __ __
4. __ __ __ ▨ __ __
5. __ __ __ __ ▨ __ __
6. __ __ __ ▨ __ __ __
7. __ __ __ __ ▨ __ __ __
8. __ __ __ ▨ __ __
9. __ __ __ __ ▨ __ __ __
10. __ __ ▨ __ __ __
11. __ __ __ ▨ __ __ __ __

What did pioneers use to read at night? _____

Name _____

Use a word from the box to complete each sentence. Then write the number of syllables in the word.

flashlight	forever	homework	inside	lifeboats	midnight
photograph	seaworthy	shipwreck	underwater	waterproof	westbound

1. In 1912, a British ship named the Titanic set sail _____ from England to New York City. _____

2. People thought the Titanic was so _____ that nothing could ever sink it. _____

3. Just before _____, the Titanic rammed an iceberg and the ship began to take on water. _____

4. Over two thousand people tried to crowd into the _____. _____

5. The ship sank in the North Atlantic Ocean, and many thought it was lost _____. _____

6. Today the Titanic is a _____ off the coast of Newfoundland. _____

7. In 1985, scientists sent an _____ robot to look at the sunken Titanic. _____

8. This small robot could explore _____ the ship. _____

9. The robot, named J.J., was equipped with a _____ camera. _____

10. The robot also had a special _____ that lit up the dark water. _____

11. J.J.'s camera took a _____ of the sunken ship. _____

12. I will write a report about the Titanic for my _____ assignment. _____

Unit 4: Reading Compound Words in Context

AT HOME

Ask your child to make a list of five compound words and use each in a sentence.

Read each word. Write each word and draw a line to divide it into syllables.

1. cable _____
2. sparkle _____
3. handle _____
4. tickle _____
5. crackle _____
6. table _____
7. puzzle _____
8. bicycle _____
9. topple _____
10. beetle _____
11. tackle _____
12. turtle _____
13. circle _____
14. whistle _____
15. battle _____
16. cuddle _____
17. title _____
18. bottle _____
19. bridle _____
20. juggle _____

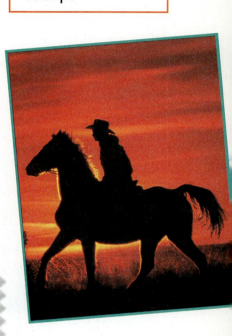

Read the clues. Use words from the box to complete the puzzle.

Across
2. It's green and sour.
4. not busy
8. fall
9. Thread goes through it.
10. the center

Down
1. weak
2. a mud _____
3. Wranglers round them up.
5. can do it
6. not rough
7. A cowhand sits in it.

| able | cattle | feeble | gentle | idle | middle |
| needle | pickle | puddle | saddle | tumble | |

Name _____

Choose a word from the box to complete each sentence. Write the word on the line.

bugle	bundle	enjoyable	giggle	little	nibble
saddle	startle	stumbled	terrible	trouble	tumbled

1. Ellen's Uncle Dave told _____ stories about things that happened long ago.

2. Some of his tall tales were a _____ far-fetched for me to believe.

3. He told Ellen about Uncle Bob, a gold miner who got into _____ with a bear.

4. Uncle Bob tied his supplies in a _____ and rode his mule west to California.

5. He also took a shiny brass _____ with him, but he couldn't play it.

6. One day, his mule _____ on the rocks while they were crossing a mountain stream.

7. The mule's _____ slipped, and Uncle Bob's supplies fell into the water.

8. Just then, a bear waded into the stream and began to _____ some fish.

9. Uncle Bob grabbed his bugle and blew it to _____ the bear.

10. Uncle Bob made a _____ racket, and the bear ran away.

11. Then Uncle Bob gathered his supplies that had _____ into the stream and went on his way.

12. Ellen had to _____ at Uncle Dave's funny story.

AT HOME

Ask your child to tell a favorite story about a family member or friend.

Read the passage. Then answer the questions below in complete sentences.

PHONICS and READING

Time Travel

Brenda and Carlos pulled the handle toward them and shut the door. Brenda turned the little knob in a circle until it pointed to "Long Ago."

"How far back in time will we travel?" asked Carlos.

"I don't know," Brenda mumbled. "We'll find out after we step outside this time machine."

The machine gave a loud rumble and a hiss. It turned in a circle and purple smoke came out of it. Then suddenly all was quiet.

"Everything is so quiet!" whispered Brenda.

"I can only hear my feeble heartbeat," Carlos said. "Where are we? Let's go outside and take a look."

They were in the middle of a Creek village. The Creek were a group of Native Americans called Woodland Indians. This village was on a hillside. The townspeople were working. Women were planting corn in a large cornfield. Men were getting ready to go on a hunting trip.

"This is incredible!" said Carlos.

Then they realized they were standing in the middle of a circle of ten Creek children. Each child began to giggle and point at the two strangers.

"Don't say anything!" Brenda whispered. "Just smile!"

1. Where did the time machine stop?

_____

2. What did Carlos and Brenda see when they stepped outside the time machine?

_____

3. What were the townspeople doing in the village?

_____

_____

4. What did the Creek children do when they saw Brenda and Carlos?

_____

Name _____

Imagine that you and a friend travel to "Long Ago" in a time machine. Write what you might see when you step outside the time machine. The words in the box may help you.

PHONICS and WRITING

able	afterward	anyone	everybody	everything
footstep	handsome	little	middle	needle
newspaper	outside	sparkle	startle	whenever

WRITING TIP Reread your first draft carefully. Think of ways you could improve your writing.

_____

_____

_____

_____

_____

_____

_____

_____

_____

_____

Ask your child to draw a picture of where the time machine landed and to read the story aloud to you.

© Steck-Vaughn Company

Read each base word. Add s, ed, and ing to make new words.

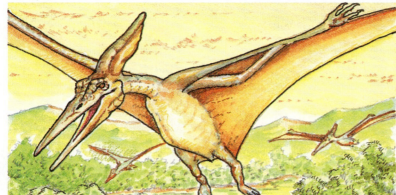

RULES If a word ends in a short vowel followed by a consonant, double the last consonant before adding an ending that begins with a vowel.

hop hop**s** hop**ped** hop**ping**

If a word ends in silent **e**, drop the **e** before adding an ending that begins with a vowel.

tame tam**es** tam**ed** tam**ing**

If a word ends in a consonant followed by **y**, change the **y** to **i** before adding **es** or **ed**. Just add **ing** to a word that ends in **y**.

fry fr**ies** fr**ied** fr**ying**

Base Word	Add s	Add ed	Add ing
1. shop			
2. flow			
3. reply			
4. glide			
5. dance			
6. try			
7. use			
8. squirt			
9. scrub			
10. divide			
11. clip			
12. dry			
13. ask			
14. hug			
15. drip			
16. study			

Name _____

1. Dinosaurs _____ Earth for more than 150 million years.

   rule
   ruled
   ruling

2. Dinosaurs _____ about 65 million years ago.

   disappear
   disappeared
   disappearing

3. Today, scientists _____ on dinosaur bones and fossils to learn what dinosaurs were like.

   rely
   relies
   relied

4. Scientists think that when dinosaurs _____ Earth, the climate was warmer than it is today.

   roam
   roamed
   roaming

5. Pterodactyls and other winged reptiles were _____ in the sky.

   fly
   flies
   flying

6. Diplodocus _____ into marshes to find plants to eat.

   wade
   waded
   wading

7. Stegosaurus would _____ attackers with its powerful, spiked tail.

   strike
   strikes
   striking

8. The impact of a meteor may have _____ the dinosaurs to become extinct.

   cause
   caused
   causing

9. Some scientists are _____ that birds are the descendants of dinosaurs.

   convince
   convinced
   convincing

10. Can you imagine what it would be like to see a

    _____ dinosaur?

    lives
    lived
    living

Ask your child to write a sentence about dinosaurs that uses one of the circled words on this page.

Read each base word. Add er and est to make new words.

Base Word	Add **er**	Add **est**
1. juicy	_____	_____
2. fast	_____	_____
3. windy	_____	_____
4. tame	_____	_____
5. flat	_____	_____
6. happy	_____	_____
7. cold	_____	_____
8. red	_____	_____
9. wet	_____	_____
10. pale	_____	_____
11. sad	_____	_____
12. messy	_____	_____
13. hot	_____	_____
14. late	_____	_____
15. funny	_____	_____

Name _____

Read the base word at the left of each sentence. Add **er** or **est** to the base word to complete the sentence. Write the word on the line.

1. **close**   Today, the _____ living relatives to dinosaurs are birds, alligators, and crocodiles.

2. **big**   The _____ the meat-eating dinosaur was, the larger was the animal it hunted.

3. **smart**   Some scientists think Troodont was one of the _____ dinosaurs because it had a big brain.

4. **small**   The _____ known adult dinosaur was Compsognathus, which was less than three feet long.

5. **tiny**   Someday scientists may discover an even _____ dinosaur.

6. **early**   The _____ dinosaur bone discovery was made in 1822 in Sussex, England.

7. **old**   The _____ known dinosaur fossils are from Eorapter, which lived about 225 million years ago in South America.

8. **large**   Thecodonts, the ancestors of dinosaurs, were no _____ than turkeys.

9. **heavy**   The _____ of the pterosaurs, or flying reptiles, had a wingspan of up to 25 feet.

10. **high**   Apatosaurus had a very long neck that helped it reach

_____ for food than Stegosaurus could reach.

11. **long**   Tyrannosaurus rex may have had the _____ teeth of any dinosaur.

12. **scary**   Which dinosaur do you think is the _____ of them all?

Unit 4: Reading Inflectional Endings
-*er* and -*est* in Context

AT HOME

Ask your child to compare two favorite dinosaurs.

Read each word below. Write the plural form of each word on the line.

1. ax   _____

2. fox   _____

3. guess   _____

4. watch   _____

5. wish   _____

6. robin   _____

7. thing   _____

8. bus   _____

9. brush   _____

10. peach   _____

11. waltz   _____

12. glass   _____

13. buzz   _____

14. tax   _____

Complete each sentence with a plural word from above.

15. Did you know that people today do the same _____ that people did long ago?

16. Pioneers used _____ to chop down trees.

17. Pioneer children liked to eat juicy _____.

18. People have paid _____ for thousands of years.

19. People in Europe have always welcomed the return

of the _____ in the spring.

20. Children have always made _____ on stars.

21. People have danced _____ for hundreds of years.

22. Ben Franklin wore _____ more than two hundred years ago.

23. I wonder how long people have used _____ to tell time.

Name _____

Read each word below. Write the plural form of each word on the line.

RULES If a word ends in a consonant followed by **y,** make it plural by changing the **y** to **i** and adding **es.** If a word ends in a vowel followed by **y,** just add **s** to make it plural.

pupp**y**	pupp**ies**
ke**y**	key**s**

1. daisy _____

2. chimney _____

3. monkey _____

4. day _____

5. fly _____

6. injury _____

7. buddy _____

8. tray _____

9. melody _____

10. beauty _____

11. pastry _____

12. turkey _____

Write the plural form of each word at the left.

13. **holiday**   During our school _____, I spend hours reading in the library.

14. **story**   I read _____ about children who lived in Canada in the 1600s.

15. **cowboy**   If you like the Wild West, you can find

    information about _____.

16. **country**   The library has books that tell what it was like to live

    in many different _____ long ago.

17. **hobby**   One of my favorite _____ is to read books about people who lived during World War II.

18. **library**   _____ are good places to find out about how people lived long ago.

© Steck-Vaughn Company

The plural words at the left have scrambled letters. Unscramble each word and write it on the line. Then draw a line to connect each plural word with the singular word that matches it at the right.

1. voheso   _____   thief

2. valehs   _____   wife

3. sleevs   _____   shelf

4. visel   _____   self

5. lowevs   _____   life

6. evwis   _____   loaf

7. levhess   _____   hoof

8. heetvis   _____   half

9. salvoe   _____   wolf

Complete each sentence with a word from the box. Make each word plural before you write it on the line.

| calf | half | knife | leaf | life | loaf | self | shelf |

Today, most people buy _____ of bread at the supermarket.

Long ago, people had to bake bread themselves or buy it from a baker. Bakers

mixed and kneaded the bread dough. Sometimes they would knead the

_____ of flavorful herbs into the dough. Then they separated the

dough into two parts and placed both _____ in pans to rise. After

the bread had baked in an oven, it was set on _____ to cool.

Then bakers used special _____ to slice the bread. Some bakers

devoted their _____ to baking the tastiest bread in town.

Name _____

Write the plural of each word below. Then find and circle the plural words in the puzzle. The words can go across, down, up, or diagonally.

RULE If a word ends in **o**, usually add **s** to make the word plural. For some words, such as **potato**, **tomato**, and **hero**, add **es** to form the plural.

radi**o**	radi**os**
tomat**o**	tomat**oes**

1. buffalo _____

2. rodeo _____

3. lasso _____

4. potato _____

5. photo _____

6. hero _____

7. kangaroo _____

8. taco _____

9. piano _____

10. banjo _____

b	u	f	f	a	l	o	e	s	k	s
g	l	p	t	f	n	m	i	k	a	s
d	a	h	b	a	n	j	o	s	n	o
z	s	o	o	c	c	e	e	f	g	t
a	s	t	h	e	r	o	e	s	a	s
q	o	o	l	n	t	n	s	c	r	o
m	s	s	i	a	r	o	d	e	o	s
m	o	r	t	w	h	l	o	s	o	u
w	k	o	p	i	a	n	o	s	s	o
b	p	o	g	h	g	a	s	s	o	s

Complete each sentence with a word from above.

11. _____ have been popular in the West for more than a hundred years.

12. Riders try their skill at roping bulls with _____ .

13. The food sold at a rodeo is good, especially the meat-filled _____ .

14. Pepperoni pizza and French fried _____ are also for sale.

15. The photographer from a newspaper takes lots of _____ of the winners.

16. The riders and ropers who win the events are treated as _____ .

© Steck-Vaughn Company

AT HOME

Ask your child to make a list of words that end in **o**. Then help your child form the plural of each word.

Read the words below. Write the plural of each word on the line.

1. tooth _____

2. man _____

3. woman _____

4. ox _____

5. moose _____

6. goose _____

7. foot _____

8. elk _____

9. salmon _____

10. cattle _____

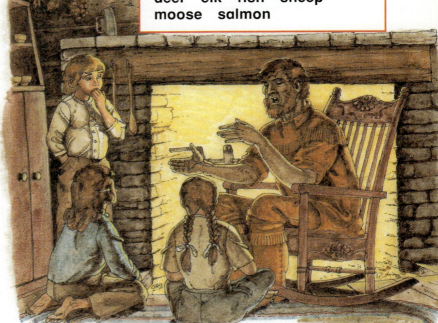

Complete each sentence with a word at the right. Write the word on the line.

11. Long ago, _____ did not have televisions.   child   children

12. An old man or _____ might tell them a story late at night.   woman   women

13. People would sit at the storyteller's _____.   foot   feet

14. Some stories were about hunting salmon, elk,

    and _____.   goose   geese

15. Some stories were tall tales about _____.   woodsmen   woodsman

16. Some stories were even about a family

    of _____.   mouse   mice

Name _____

Read each sentence. Circle the word that completes the sentence. Write the word on the line.

1. Life must have been very different before people had televisions,

   telephones, and _____.

   radio
   radios
   radioes

2. Men rode on _____ to deliver the mail.

   pony
   ponys
   ponies

3. Ladies and _____ had to wait a long time to get news
   from far away.

   gentleman
   gentlemen
   gentlemans

4. Police blew whistles when they saw _____ robbing
   a store.

   thief
   thiefs
   thieves

5. Long ago, no one had any _____ at home, at school,
   or at work.

   computer
   computers
   computeres

6. People could not fly to faraway places on _____.

   holidays
   holidaies
   holiday

7. My favorite _____ of long ago are Chief Sitting Bull
   and Wyatt Earp.

   hero
   heros
   heroes

8. Do you think it was harder for detectives to solve _____
   before they had computers?

   mystery
   mysteries
   mysterys

9. Long ago, people baked their own _____ of fresh
   bread every day.

   loaf
   loaves
   loafs

10. A hundred years from now, _____ will study us and
    talk about how we lived long ago.

    child
    childs
    children

AT HOME

Ask your child to choose two plural words
and use them in sentences.

Read each phrase in the box. Then write the phrase in the correct column.

boys' shoes	cook's supplies
girls' jackets	horse's bridle
horses' saddles	runners' race
scout's campfire	team's caps

RULES The **possessive** form of a word shows ownership. If there is only one owner, add an **apostrophe** and **s.** This is a **singular possessive**.

If a word is plural and ends in **s**, add an **apostrophe** after the final **s** to show there is more than one owner. This is a **plural possessive**.

the **pioneer's** horse
the **pioneers'** wagon train

Singular Possessive

_____

_____

_____

_____

Plural Possessive

_____

_____

_____

_____

Change each singular possessive phrase below into a plural possessive phrase. Write each phrase on the line.

1. wagon's wheels _____

2. boy's clothes _____

3. man's shovels _____

4. driver's gloves _____

5. coyote's howls _____

6. family's pets _____

7. miner's mules _____

8. scout's maps _____

9. mountain's trails _____

10. river's bends _____

Name _____

Look at the map of the Oregon Trail. Then read the sentences below. Circle the word that completes each sentence. Write it on the line.

MINNESOTA TERRITORY

Missouri R.

UNORGANIZED TERRITORY

Missouri R.

IOWA

Fort Kearny

MISSOURI

Independence Missouri

Fort Vancouver

Columbia R.

OREGON TRAIL

OREGON TERRITORY

Fort Boise

Fort Hall

Snake R.

Sublette's Cutoff

Fort Laramie

OREGON TRAIL

PACIFIC OCEAN

CALIFORNIA

CALIFORNIA TRAIL

UTAH TERRITORY

SPANISH TRAIL

1. In the 1840s and 1850s, _____ wagons headed west on the Oregon Trail.

   pioneer's   pioneers'

2. Explorers, fur trappers, and _____ were the first people to use the route.

   trader's   traders

3. The rich farmland of _____ Willamette Valley attracted many pioneers.

   Oregon's   Oregon

4. Many _____ futures depended on the success of the trip.

   family's   families'

5. The pioneers gathered food and other _____ for the journey.

   supplies   supply's

6. Some families went south when they reached _____ Cutoff.

   Sublette's   Sublettes'

7. The _____ final trail followed along the Columbia River.

   journeys'   journey's

8. People loaded their supplies and animals onto rafts at the _____ banks.

   rivers'   river's

9. By 1846, more than six thousand _____ lives had changed.

   people's   peoples'

10. When the coast-to-coast railroad opened in 1869, the Oregon

    _____ importance ended.

    Trail's   Trails'

Unit 4: Reading Singular and Plural Possessives in Context

AT HOME

Ask your child to choose one of the words above and use it in a sentence.

© Steck-Vaughn Company

Write a contraction for each pair of words below.

1. should not _____
2. would have _____
3. you are _____
4. he is _____
5. have not _____
6. do not _____
7. she will _____
8. they have _____
9. does not _____
10. they are _____
11. are not _____
12. could not _____

Circle the contraction in each sentence. Write the two words it stands for on the line.

13. I wonder what it would've been like to live in the Stone Age. _____

14. I'll bet we would have seen many strange animals. _____

15. I've read about woolly mammoths that roamed the area. _____

16. Saber-toothed tigers lived then, too, but they're extinct now. _____

17. Today, we don't have to worry about mastodons, either. _____

18. Let's find some books in the library about prehistoric times. _____

Name _____

Make a contraction from the words at the right. Write it on the line to complete each sentence.

1. Cave dwellers _____ write down important events on paper.

   did not

2. _____ studied ancient drawings painted on cave walls.

   We have

3. _____ interesting to look at drawings from long ago.

   It is

4. _____ a great work of art?

   What is

5. _____ take a look at the art Michelangelo created.

   Let us

6. My teacher says that _____ a great artist.

   he is

7. _____ show you examples of masks made by Native Americans.

   I will

8. Most societies _____ created art to decorate their homes.

   would have

9. On our trip to the museum, _____ see art from times past.

   we will

10. We will go when _____ ready.

   you are

Write contractions for the following words.

11. they will _____   12. should have _____

13. they have _____   14. had not _____

15. would not _____   16. does not _____

17. cannot _____   18. we are _____

19. are not _____   20. will not _____

21. you will _____   22. I am _____

AT HOME

Ask your child to choose a contraction and use it in a sentence.

PHONICS and SPELLING

In each sentence below, the word **dinosaur** stands for a word in the box. Replace the word **dinosaur** with the correct word. Write each word at the bottom of the page.

babies	bicycles	chalkboard	didn't	earliest	family's
handlebars	larger	puddles	racing	shopping	
stories	studied	thousands	tumbling	wasn't	

1. Our class dinosaur about the history of transportation.

2. We learned about the first two-wheeled dinosaur.

3. Our teacher drew several early models on the dinosaur.

4. The dinosaur two-wheeled bicycle was built in 1818.

5. It was called a draisienne, and it dinosaur have any pedals.

6. It dinosaur until 1861 that Pierre Michaux and his son Ernest made the first real bicycle.

7. People called the dinosaur invention the boneshaker because it was rough to ride.

8. Soon, people were dinosaur their bikes between Paris and Rouen.

9. There are many dinosaur about early bicycles.

10. Some early bicycles had a small back wheel and a much dinosaur front wheel.

11. These bikes were popular, even though riders risked dinosaur from such a height.

12. Early bikes didn't have fenders, so riders who rode through dinosaur got wet.

13. Dinosaur of people began to use bicycles for transportation.

14. Some people put a basket in front of the dinosaur so they could carry things.

15. With a basket, they could carry dinosaur bags or tools.

16. Today, some parents carry their dinosaur in special seats on the back of their bikes.

1. _____   2. _____   3. _____   4. _____

5. _____   6. _____   7. _____   8. _____

9. _____   10. _____   11. _____   12. _____

13. _____   14. _____   15. _____   16. _____

Name _____

Unit 4: Spelling Compounds, Contractions, Plurals, *-le,* and Word Endings

Read the clues. Find the words from the box that answer the clues and circle them in the puzzle. These words can go down, across, or diagonally.

1. two words for *didn't*
2. opposite of *shorter*
3. to scare or surprise
4. the very smallest
5. a bird that sings
6. more than one knife
7. the least wild
8. more than one mouse
9. more than one monkey
10. Batman and Superman
11. A dog's bone belongs to a _____.
12. more than one radio
13. less difficult
14. what you're doing on a mountain trail
15. French _____
16. not busy
17. more than one box
18. opposite of *outside*

boxes	did not	dog	easier	fries	heroes
hiking	idle	inside	knives	mice	monkeys
radios	songbird	startle	taller	tamest	tiniest

```
b g t a m e s t r m t s
o z h j k e j y a o i x
x p s m v d o g d n n b
e h o i m p t i i v i s
s i n c d i t r o e e t
o k g e c y c l s y s a
i i b e d i d n o t t r
n n i h e r o e s f n t
s g r i d l e p i r e l
i g d e a s i e r i g e
d m o n k e y s o e y r
e t a l l e r o p s p p
```

Unit 4: Syllables, Compounds, Contractions, Plurals, *-le,* and Word Endings Review

Ask your child to choose two words from the box and use them in a sentence.

Read the passage. Then answer the questions below in complete sentences.

PHONICS and READING

The Boy King

He was called the Boy King because he was nine years old when he became pharaoh, or king, of all Egypt. His name was Tutankhamen, (too-tahng-KAH-men), but we call him King Tut. He lived about 3,000 years ago and died when he was only 18 years of age.

Thousands of years ago, pharaohs were buried underground in Egypt's Valley of the Kings. More than sixty tombs are known, but some are easier to find than others. Archaeologists, people who study past human life, first thought that all the tombs had been robbed long ago, but they were wrong. Thieves hadn't found the door to King Tut's tomb. The door was hidden under rock chips dumped from the digging of another tomb.

In 1922, an archaeologist named Howard Carter entered the tomb of King Tut. He made the biggest discovery of his life. He found richer treasures than he could ever imagine sparkling inside the burial chamber. There were thousands of incredible objects, including a solid gold coffin, a gold mask, and King Tut's jewelry. The discovery helped us know more about the pharaohs' lives.

1. Why was King Tut called the Boy King?

    _____

2. Who was buried in the Valley of the Kings?

    _____

3. Why was King Tut's tomb saved?

    _____

    _____

4. What did Howard Carter find in the tomb?

    _____

5. Why was Howard Carter's discovery so important?

    _____

    _____

Name _____

Unit 4: Reading Syllables, Compounds, Contractions,
Plurals, *-le,* and Word Endings in Context

Imagine that you are a reporter who is going to interview King Tut. Write four questions you would ask him. Then write King Tut's answers to your questions. The words in the box may help you.

PHONICS and WRITING

biggest	didn't	families
famous	forever	golden
happiest	lives	puzzle
replied	robbing	stories
thousand	weren't	wishes

WRITING TIP After you have revised your first draft, ask a classmate to read it. Your classmate can help you decide whether your draft needs more revision.

Unit 4: Writing Syllables, Compounds, Contractions, Plurals, *-le,* and Word Endings

AT HOME

Have your child read the questions and answers to you.

Read each sentence. Circle the word at the right that completes each sentence. Write the word on the line.

Unit 4
CHECK-UP

1. Before people learned to write, there _____ an easy way to record history.

won't
wasn't
didn't

2. Ancient artists drew pictures of _____ and bison on cave walls.

horse's
horses
horses'

3. Mom was going to bring home pictures of prehistoric cave art, but she left her _____ at work.

breakfast
briefcase
bubble

4. The rain made it a _____ day for a soccer game.

tremble
triangle
terrible

5. The _____ basketball team is the best in the state.

girls
girls'
girl's

6. Our team was ahead in both _____ of the game.

halves
halfs
half's

7. An old-fashioned word for _____ is *spectacles*.

glass
glass's
glasses

8. Our cat scares the _____ away from the house.

mices
mice
mouse's

9. I can lift a _____ weight than my little brother can.

heavy
heaviest
heavier

10. Dan is always _____ in his journal.

writing
write
writes

Name _____

Fill in the circle next to the word that completes the sentence.

1. Ancient humans sewed with _____ made of bone.
   - ○ needs
   - ○ needles
   - ○ needy
   - ○ needless

2. For hundreds of years, people have used _____ to walk on the Arctic snow.
   - ○ snowshoes
   - ○ snowdrifts
   - ○ snowflakes
   - ○ snowmen

3. The trackers followed the wolf pack by listening for the _____ howls.
   - ○ wolfs'
   - ○ wolve's
   - ○ wolves'
   - ○ wolve

4. Long ago, painters had to make their own _____ out of animal hair.
   - ○ brushes
   - ○ brushed
   - ○ brushs
   - ○ brushing

5. Wagon trains _____ to make it over the mountains before the winter snows came.
   - ○ tries
   - ○ trying
   - ○ tryed
   - ○ tried

6. The lookouts on the Titanic _____ see the iceberg until it was too late.
   - ○ doesn't
   - ○ shouldn't
   - ○ didn't
   - ○ isn't

7. Our class is learning about how Chinese _____ lived long ago.
   - ○ childs
   - ○ childrens
   - ○ child's
   - ○ children

8. Ellen's family was so large that her mom cooked two _____ for Thanksgiving dinner.
   - ○ turkies
   - ○ turkeys
   - ○ turkey
   - ○ turkey's

9. Always set the table with plates, forks, spoons, _____, glasses, and napkins.
   - ○ knives
   - ○ knifes
   - ○ knife's
   - ○ knive

10. The bones of Eorapter are the _____ known dinosaur fossils.
    - ○ oldest
    - ○ old
    - ○ older
    - ○ older'

Do Spiders Stick to Their Own Webs?

The spider weaves a sticky web
To capture bugs to eat.
What keeps the spider's sticky web
From sticking to her feet?

Spider webs are very tricky
Because not all the strands are sticky.
Unlike the passing hapless fly,
The spider knows which strands are dry.

But if she accidentally stands
Upon one of the sticky strands,
She still would not get stuck, you see —
Her oily body slides off free.

Amy Goldman Koss

Think About It

Why don't spiders stick to their webs?
What other mysteries of nature can you think of?

121

Dear Family of _____,

Your child will be learning about suffixes, prefixes, and base words. Your child will be using these skills to read about the theme of Nature's Mysteries. Here are some activities you can do together.

- Make a list of these base words: *wash, spoon, soft, slow, leak, elect, west, sing,* and *danger.* Have your child make new words by adding one of the following suffixes to the base words: *-y, -ly, -ful, -ness, -ous, -ion, -er, -able, -ward.* Ask your child to write the new words.

- Play a game of Concentration with ten pairs of index cards. With your child, think of ten different words with prefixes. Write a base word on one card of each pair. On the matching card, write the base word with a prefix added to it, such as *cycle* and *tricycle* or *western* and *midwestern.* Shuffle the cards and place each face down on a table. Take turns trying to turn over a matching pair of cards.

- Cut out a variety of circles from colored construction paper. On each circle, write a base word, a prefix, or a suffix, such as the base word *predict,* the prefix *un-,* and the suffix *-able.* Mix up all the circles and have your child choose circles to make caterpillars that form words with prefixes and suffixes. Have your child finish each caterpillar by adding a head.

LIBRARY LINK

You might like to visit the library and find the book *How Bats "See" in the Dark* by Malcolm Penny. Read it with your child.

Estimada familia de _____,

Su niño o niña aprenderá sufijos, prefijos y palabras base en inglés. Él o ella usará estos conocimientos en su lectura sobre los Misterios de la naturaleza. Algunas actividades que usted y su niño o niña pueden hacer en inglés aparecen a continuación.

- Haga una lista de las siguientes palabras base: *wash, spoon, soft, slow, leak, elect, west, sing* y *danger.* Pídale a su niño o niña que construya palabras nuevas añadiendo uno de los siguientes sufijos a las palabras base: *-y, -ly, -ful, -ness, -ous, -ion, -er, -able, -ward.* Dígale a su niño o niña que escriba las palabras.

- Jueguen al juego de Concentración con diez pares de tarjetas. Juntos piensen en diez palabras distintas con prefijos. Escriban una palabra base en una tarjeta de cada par. En la otra tarjeta, escriban la palabra base añadiéndole un prefijo, como *cycle* y *tricycle* o *western* y *midwestern.* Baraje las tarjetas y póngalas boca abajo en la mesa. Túrnense tratando de volver boca arriba un par de tarjetas que correspondan, como se demuestra en el dibujo de arriba.

- Recorten una variedad de círculos de papel grueso de diferente colores. En cada círculo, escriba una palabra base, un prefijo o un sufijo, como la palabra base *predict,* el prefijo *un-* y el sufijo *-able.* Mezclen todos los círculos y pídale a su niño o niña que escoja círculos para construir orugas que formen palabras con prefijos y sufijos. Pídale a su niño o niña que complete cada oruga añadiéndole una cabeza.

Add the suffix in dark print to each word in the row to make new words.

1. **y** luck _____ leak _____

2. **ly** neat _____ kind _____

3. **ful** care _____ play _____

4. **ness** soft _____ clever _____

5. **less** seed _____ tooth _____

Here's a mystery of nature for you. Look at the close-up of this animal. What is it? Answer each clue below. Read the letters in the shaded box to solve the puzzle.

1. being clever   __ __ __ ▢ __ __ __

2. without care   __ __ __ ▢ __ __ __

3. having a chill   __ __ __ ▢ __ __

4. full of flavor   __ __ __ ▢ __ __ __

5. in a serious way   __ ▢ __ __ __ __ __

6. having haste   __ __ __ ▢ __

7. having a leak   __ __ __ __ ▢

It's a _____ tree ant.

Name _____

Read the base words and suffixes below. Write the new words.

1. easy + ly = _____

2. health + y = _____

3. fear + ful = _____

4. glad + ly = _____

5. scare + y = _____

6. sugar + y = _____

7. close + ly = _____

8. count + less = _____

9. soft + ness = _____

10. crab + y = _____

11. spice + y = _____

12. forget + ful = _____

13. fond + ness = _____

14. noise + y = _____

Complete each sentence with a word from the list above.

15. Have you ever looked _____ at insects?

16. I am _____ that my dog will get ticks or fleas again.

17. After walks in the park, my dog has gotten ticks _____ times.

18. I don't have a _____ for ticks and fleas!

19. The vet is amazed at how _____ my dog is.

20. I am not _____ about taking care of my pets.

Unit 5: Suffixes *-less, -ness, -ful, -ly,* and *-y*

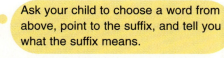

AT HOME

Ask your child to choose a word from above, point to the suffix, and tell you what the suffix means.

Use the base words and suffixes to make new words. Complete the puzzle using words from the list.

1. elect + ion = _____

2. amuse + ment = _____

3. fury + ous = _____

4. bright + en = _____

5. create + ion = _____

6. enjoy + ment = _____

7. act + ion = _____

8. educate + ion = _____

9. danger + ous = _____

10. short + en = _____

Across

3. the act of creating

5. full of danger

7. the act of educating

8. to become short

9. the result of enjoying

Down

1. to become bright

2. the act of electing

4. full of fury

6. the result of acting

Name _____

**Circle the word that completes each sentence.
Write the word on the line.**

1. Stan noticed something very _____ about the fish in the stream near his house.

   mystery
   mysterious
   mindful

2. A new housing _____ was being built nearby.

   development
   develop
   develops

3. Most of the fish in the stream had disappeared, and

   Stan was _____.

   suspicious
   suspect
   suspended

4. Stan cared about fish, plants, and birds in his

   _____.

   envious
   environment
   envelope

5. He tested the water and found that _____ was why the fish were disappearing.

   pollutes
   pollution
   polluting

6. He found _____ chemicals in the water.

   poisonous
   pavement
   protection

7. Stan decided to take _____.

   admit
   action
   amusement

8. Stan had a _____ with nature and what it needs to survive.

   fascinate
   fascination
   fulfillment

9. Stan asked the city council to sign an

   _____ to clean up the water pollution.

   argument
   agreement
   agent

10. Stan hopes that soon many fish will _____ the stream again.

    brighten
    brighter
    brightly

AT HOME

Ask your child to write three sentences about what can be done to keep streams clean.

The words in the box are hidden in the puzzle. Circle each word you find. Words can go down, across, or diagonally. Then write each word on the correct line below.

s	b	g	p	m	k	s	b	c	y	g	v	c
b	l	o	o	o	g	h	g	o	l	f	e	r
c	o	n	x	m	p	i	i	n	l	n	f	e
v	a	a	v	e	f	p	b	d	n	s	a	a
i	n	r	e	e	r	p	e	u	c	c	r	t
o	p	i	t	c	h	e	r	c	h	u	m	o
l	o	p	o	o	k	r	h	t	e	l	e	r
i	e	d	i	t	o	r	v	o	m	p	r	i
n	m	n	n	b	v	n	b	r	i	t	s	s
i	w	r	i	t	e	r	i	s	s	o	t	q
s	s	c	i	e	n	t	i	s	t	r	r	r
t	p	i	s	t	i	s	t	r	t	p	w	x

boxer
cartoonist
chemist
conductor
creator
editor
farmer
golfer
pitcher
scientist
sculptor
shipper
violinist
writer

1. someone who pitches baseballs

    _____

2. someone who boxes in a ring

    _____

3. someone who writes books

    _____

4. someone who draws cartoons

    _____

5. someone who mixes chemicals

    _____

6. someone who studies science

    _____

7. someone who ships packages

    _____

8. someone who golfs

    _____

9. someone who conducts music

    _____

10. someone who farms

    _____

11. someone who creates

    _____

12. someone who plays the violin

    _____

13. someone who edits books

    _____

14. someone who sculpts

    _____

Name _____

1. Every fall when the days _____,
   many birds begin to fly south.   shortly   shorten   shortness

2. _____ who study birds are
   called ornithologists.   Scientists Scientific Senseless

3. In the spring, you can hear flocks of

   _____ birds return north. nosy   noisy   noiseless

4. This movement back and forth is called

   bird _____.   migration migrate   mighty

5. Birds fly _____ miles over
   rivers, mountains, and oceans.   countless counting   county

6. Scientists wanted to know how birds find their

   way in the _____ of night. darkly   darken   darkness

7. They conducted an _____.   action   expert   experiment

8. They put some birds inside a dark planetarium

   with _____ shining stars.   brighten brightly   brightest

9. The birds flew in one _____. direction directly director

10. The scientists were _____ to
    change the position of the stars in the planetarium. careful careless career

11. _____, the birds changed
    their direction, too!   Suddenly   Sunrise   Southward

12. I have a _____ for watching birds. found fondly fondness

AT HOME

Ask your child to tell you two facts about
bird migration.

Add the suffix in dark print to each word in the row to make new words.

> **RULE** Remember, a suffix changes the meaning of a word.
> **able** means "able to be"
>   wash**able** = able to be washed
> **age** means "collection of" or "process"
>   bagg**age** = collection of bags
> **ance** means "quality of" or "process"
>   guid**ance** = the process of guiding
> **ward** means "in the direction of"
>   east**ward** = in the direction of east

1. **able** profit _____ enjoy _____

2. **age** pass _____ store _____

3. **ance** assist _____ insure _____

4. **ward** west _____ up _____

Complete each sentence with a word that you wrote above.

5. Josita thinks it's _____ to gather mysterious facts about animals.

6. She knows a puma is capable of leaping 23 feet _____ into a tree.

7. Josita asks for _____ from the librarian to find animal facts.

8. The Lamas family traveled _____ from Chicago to Los Angeles.

Puma

9. When a store makes a lot of money, we say it is _____.

10. Health _____ is a good thing to have when you are sick.

11. An underground _____ connects the two buildings.

12. My summer clothes are packed away in _____.

Name _____

Read each word. Write each word and draw a line to divide it into syllables.

1. action _____

2. importance _____

3. broken _____

4. preservation _____

5. careful _____

6. scientists _____

7. dangerous _____

8. sticky _____

9. downward _____

10. storage _____

Complete each sentence with a word from the list above.

11. The tar pits in Los Angeles were once a _____ place for animals.

12. As animals came to drink the water in the tar pits, they became trapped in the _____ tar.

13. No _____ could free the animal, and it died.

14. When the bones became soaked with tar, they sank _____ to the bottom of the pit.

15. The oily tar ensured the _____ of the bones for thousands of years.

16. In 1906, Dr. John Merriam found bones from a giant ground sloth, and realized their _____.

17. _____ study the fossils to unlock the mysteries of the past.

18. The bones are often _____ into many small pieces.

19. Scientists have to be very _____ as they put the bones together.

20. After the bones are sorted, they are put into trays and labeled for _____.

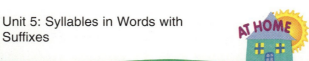

AT HOME

Ask your child to tell you how many syllables are in each word in the list above.

© Steck-Vaughn Company

Find the hidden word in the letters that follow each sentence. Write each word on the line.

PHONICS and SPELLING

actor	basement	darkness	dentist
election	furious	guidance	helpful
kicker	lighten	sleepy	slowly
storage	toothless	washable	westward

1. This is the state of being dark. hdrarakbneisys _____

2. It's full of help. ehlelqpfqull _____

3. This rhymes with *curious*. ufouwrpioaus _____

4. This means "without a tooth." toeotrhlsesse _____

5. It's how you feel when you go to bed. xspleetypy _____

6. This is the opposite of *quickly*. slrowwqluy _____

7. This is the lowest level of some houses. pbsasremtent _____

8. This means "to make lighter." bleighmtnen _____

9. This is the act of electing. lelleocitiiomn _____

10. This is the name for someone who acts. satctaoars _____

11. This is someone who takes care of teeth. pdiddenteisit _____

12. This person kicks a football. kcicwkpeor _____

13. This describes something that can be washed. cwsashbaalblae _____

14. This is the process of guiding. giuildkainoce _____

15. This is the process of storing. ssggtoaraagoe _____

16. This means "in the direction of west." pwiemsitpwatrd _____

Name _____

Answer each clue with a word from the box. Write the word on the lines to the right. Then write the letters in order from 1–15 to find the answer to the question below.

argument	artist	backward	careless	director
goodness	humorous	pavement	poisonous	scary
shorten	snowy	spoonful	wavy	wobbly

1. A day of snow is _____. __ __ __ __ __
   15

2. without taking care __ __ __ __ __ __ __ __
   10

3. the result of arguing __ __ __ __ __ __ __ __
   9

4. full of poison __ __ __ __ __ __ __ __ __
   12

5. a person who directs __ __ __ __ __ __ __ __
   7

6. going back in direction __ __ __ __ __ __ __ __
   1

7. having a wobble __ __ __ __ __ __
   8

8. causing to be scared __ __ __ __ __
   2

9. to become shorter __ __ __ __ __ __ __
   3

10. having waves __ __ __ __
   6

11. full of humor __ __ __ __ __ __ __ __
   4

12. This has been paved. __ __ __ __ __ __ __ __
   5

13. a state of being good __ __ __ __ __ __ __ __
   14

14. someone who makes art __ __ __ __ __ __
   11

15. a full spoon __ __ __ __ __ __ __ __
   13

How can a spider tell if it has caught a leaf or an insect in its web? There is a way to tell the difference!

__ __   __ __ __   __ __ __ __ __ __ __ __ __ __
1 2   3 4 5   6 7 8 9 10 11 12 13 14 15

AT HOME

Ask your child to choose a word from the box and use it in a sentence.

Read the passage. Then use complete sentences to answer the questions below.

How Do Animals Talk?

We all know that animals don't speak words, but many creatures can communicate clearly with each other. How do animals "talk"?

When the arrow-poison frog senses a dangerous enemy, its colorful eyespots send a warning. "Careful, now! I'm poisonous! Leave me alone," it warns.

Animal communication can be quite noisy, too. Have you ever heard a rattlesnake's rattle? It can frighten even the bravest animal with the unforgettable message: "Stay away!" A wolf howls loudly to caution other wolves that they are trespassers on its territory. The wordless snarls of a growling grizzly bear plainly send the message: "Don't come near me, or you'll be sorry!"

When it is time to attract a mate, animals in the sea create noisy underwater entertainment. Fish called croakers give out sounds that spread outward like a chorus of croaking frogs. Ocean singers include the humpback whale, which can sing for ten to fifteen minutes at a time. The white whale, called the beluga, is nicknamed the "sea canary" because of its noisy chirps and shrill whistles.

Rattlesnake

Arrow-poison frog

1. What do an arrow-poison frog's eyespots say to its enemies?

   _____

2. Why does a rattlesnake shake its rattle?

   _____

3. What animal growls wordlessly to warn those who come too near?

   _____

4. How did the croaker get its name?

   _____

5. Why is the beluga called the "sea canary"?

   _____

Name _____

Think of a pet or another animal that you know about. Write a paragraph describing how this animal communicates with you or other animals. The words in the box may help you.

PHONICS and WRITING

action	actor	assistance
careless	comfortable	communication
disturbance	downward	enjoyable
humorous	loudness	observer
quickly	quietly	upward

> **Writing Tip** As you reread your revised draft, ask yourself whether you have expressed your ideas clearly and in a logical order.

_____

_____

_____

_____

_____

_____

_____

_____

_____

_____

AT HOME

Ask your child to read the paragraph to you.

Add the prefixes below to the words in the lists. Write each new word on the line.

RULE A **prefix** is a word part added to the beginning of a base word to change its meaning.
pre means "before"
 preteen = before teen years
re means "back" or "again"
 reread = to read again

Add pre

1. school _____

2. war _____

3. cook _____

4. heat _____

5. view _____

6. pay _____

7. historic _____

Add re

8. view _____

9. bound _____

10. appear _____

11. locate _____

12. fund _____

13. new _____

14. turn _____

Complete each sentence with a word you wrote in the lists above.

15. We went to the movies and saw a _____ of a film about nature's mysteries.

16. Did you know that salmon _____ to the place they are born when they are ready to die?

17. We find out about _____ mysteries by studying fossils.

18. I learned how to write my name when I was in _____.

19. Dad has to _____ the oven before he bakes the pizza.

20. Our school will _____ our muddy soccer field to a drier place.

21. I like to catch a _____ when I play basketball.

22. When spring comes, the leaves _____ on the trees.

23. I need to _____ my words one more time before the spelling test.

24. My radio is broken, so I want a _____ from the store.

Name _____

Add the prefixes below to the words in the lists. Write the new words on the lines.

ex

port _____

claim _____

act _____

press _____

tend _____

de

code _____

fog _____

rail _____

ice _____

press _____

un

clear _____

able _____

welcome _____

happy _____

tie _____

Answer each clue with a word from above. Write the answer in the puzzle.

Across

1. to remove the code

4. not welcome

6. to reach out

7. to press down

Down

2. to take away the fog

3. to remove the ice

4. the opposite of tie

5. to put into words

AT HOME

Ask your child to choose two words from the puzzle and use them in sentences.

Add the prefixes below to the words in the lists. Write each new word on the line.

RULE Remember, a prefix changes the meaning of a word.

sub means "under" or "less than"
  subway = a way or road that goes under the street

semi means "half" or "partly"
  semicircle = a half circle

mid means "middle"
  midday = the middle of the day

sub	**mid**	**semi**
marine _____	night _____	annual _____
zero _____	western _____	precious _____
standard _____	summer _____	private _____
soil _____	air _____	sweet _____
normal _____	way _____	final _____

Answer each clue with a word from above. Write the word on the line.

1. This word means "below the soil." _____

2. This word describes one type of chocolate. _____

3. This word means "partly precious." _____

4. This word means "in the middle of the air." _____

5. July comes around this time of year. _____

6. This temperature is very, very cold. _____

7. This kind of boat travels underwater. _____

8. This type of room is not completely private. _____

9. Ohio is a state in this region of the U.S.A. _____

10. Children should be asleep at this time. _____

Name _____

**Circle the word that completes each sentence.
Write the word on the line.**

1. It is difficult to study animals that are always _____ underwater.
   submarine   semicircle   submerged

2. Scientists have been _____ to study the mysterious giant squid.
   unveiled   unable   semiprivate

3. Scientists use a _____ to search for giant squid in the sea.
   submarine   subnormal   subway

4. Temperatures can reach _____ levels in Greenland.
   semifinal   subzero   semiprecious

5. We usually eat lunch around _____.
   midnight   midday   midway

6. My dog caught a tennis ball in _____.
   midair   midwestern   substandard

7. Our class sat around the music teacher in a _____.
   semiprecious   semicircle   misadventure

8. Illinois is a _____ state in the U.S.A.
   semiannual   subscribe   midwestern

9. It is dark and quiet in my city around _____.
   midsection   sublevel   midnight

10. We dug down three inches into the dirt to find the richer _____.
    subset   subsoil   subzero

11. An opal is a _____ stone.
    semiprivate   semiprecious   submerge

12. My family likes to sit outside on the porch in _____.
    midsummer   mideastern   midair

AT HOME

Help your child find words in magazines that
have the prefixes *mid-*, *semi-*, and *sub-*.
Discuss the meaning of each word.

Write the word from the box that answers each question.

1. What word means "having two feet"? _____

2. What word means "able to speak two languages"? _____

3. What has three wheels? _____

4. What is a stand with three legs called? _____

5. What is an area that includes three states? _____

6. What do we call something that shares two cultures? _____

7. What is a type of plane with two-part wings? _____

8. What word means "having three colors"? _____

9. What word means "every two months"? _____

10. What word means "every three weeks"? _____

11. What is a group of three books or movies called? _____

12. What word means "every two weeks"? _____

> **RULE** Remember, a prefix changes the meaning of a word.
> **bi** means "two"
>   **bi**cycle = a cycle with two wheels
> **tri** means "three"
>   **tri**angle = a shape with three angles

bicultural
bilingual
bimonthly
biped
biplane
biweekly
tricolor
tricycle
trilogy
tripod
tristate
triweekly

Complete each sentence with a word from the box above.

13. The scientists took a _____ to the Arctic to study the mysterious habits of wolves.

14 A photographer put his camera on a three-legged stand called a _____.

15. My little sister just learned how to ride a _____.

16. On our vacation, we traveled over a _____ area.

17. Since Elena speaks Spanish and English, she is _____.

Name _____

Circle the prefixes in the words. Then write each word in the correct column below.

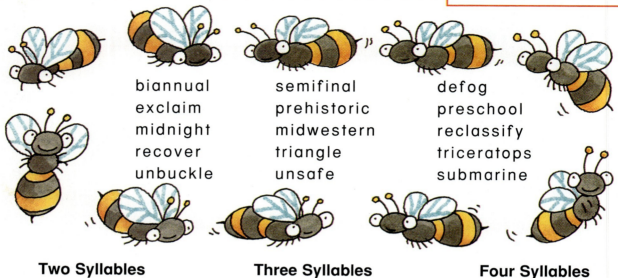

biannual   semifinal   defog
exclaim   prehistoric   preschool
midnight   midwestern   reclassify
recover   triangle   triceratops
unbuckle   unsafe   submarine

Two Syllables   **Three Syllables**   **Four Syllables**

_____   _____   _____

_____   _____   _____

_____   _____   _____

_____   _____   _____

_____   _____   _____

Read the paragraph below. Circle each word that has two syllables. Underline each word that has three syllables.

Would you expect a honeybee to dance? It certainly does! First, a honeybee flies away to look for nectar. When it returns to the hive, it dances for the other bees. This dance tells the honeybees exactly where the food is, what kind of food it is, and even how good the food tastes! The dancing bee repeats the same dance over and over. Worker bees touch the dancer to feel its vibrations. Then the other bees respond by flying away to follow the dancer's directions!

AT HOME

Ask your child to find two words in a newspaper with prefixes he or she has learned and tell how many syllables each word has.

Circle the prefix in each word. Use the rules to write a short definition of each word.

RULE Remember, a prefix changes the meaning of a word.
dis means "not" or "the opposite of"
  dishonest = not honest
mis means "wrong" or "bad"
  misplaced = in the wrong place
non means "not" or "without"
  nonstop = without stopping

1. mistreat _____

2. nonskid _____

3. disagree _____

4. misprint _____

5. nonsmoking _____

6. misdirect _____

7. misadventure _____

8. disloyal _____

9. nonsense _____

10. disappear _____

11. nonpoisonous _____

12. misguided _____

Complete each sentence with a word from the list above.

13. We must protect the rain forests so that they won't _____.

14. I think building large cities in the middle of a jungle is _____.

15. Why would anyone _____ with the idea of protecting nature?

16. Poisonous or _____, all snakes need to be protected from people.

17. I try not to _____ any living creature or plant.

18. It would be a _____ to get lost in a tropical rain forest.

Name _____

Circle the word that completes each sentence. Write the word on the line.

1. Do you think animals can _____ when an earthquake is coming?

   predict
   refund
   reward

2. Scientists think _____ animal behavior may be a way to predict earthquakes.

   preteen
   unusual
   repeat

3. Before an earthquake in Italy, hundreds of cats _____ from the area.

   disagreed
   disappeared
   mistreated

4. In Japan in 1974, snakes crawled out of hibernation holes _____ two months before an earthquake.

   exchange
   decode
   exactly

5. It is _____ whether animals have some way of telling if an earthquake will happen.

   unclear
   nonskid
   discharge

6. Some animals _____ to many events in strange ways.

   refund
   react
   unfair

7. Scientists continue to _____ reports of strange animal behavior that takes place before earthquakes.

   review
   example
   prevent

8. My dad had to _____ the car windows before we could leave.

   preschool
   relocate
   defrost

9. If you _____ your books, they will not last very long.

   mistake
   mistreat
   unsafe

10. An athlete who competes in three events is called a _____.

    triathlete
    trio
    tripod

AT HOME

Ask your child to choose one word that is not circled and use it in a sentence.

© Steck-Vaughn Company

Circle the prefixes in the words below. Then read the clues in the puzzle. Unscramble the letters to find a word from the list that answers each clue.

coeditor   codirect   compact

compile   compose   compound

condense   confirm   conserve

conspire   contest   cooperate

cosign   costar   compare

1. to sign with someone else   ginocs   _____

2. to save   veernocs   _____

3. to write music   moosepc   _____

4. to star with someone else   troacs   _____

5. small   moccapt   _____

6. to put together   milecop   _____

7. to direct a play with a partner   reccotid   _____

8. to make sure   mircfon   _____

9. to work together   praceetoo   _____

10. to study two things together   pearmco   _____

Name _____

**Draw lines to divide each word into syllables.
Then write each word in the correct column below.**

> **RULE** If a word has a prefix, divide the word between the prefix and the base word. Some prefixes, such as **semi,** have two syllables.

coeditors   combination   compare

condense   confirm   conservation

disagree   discolor   discomfort

midair   midsummer   mispronounce

misunderstood   nonsense   semicircle

Two Syllables	**Three Syllables**	**Four Syllables**
_____	_____	_____
_____	_____	_____
_____	_____	_____
_____	_____	_____
_____	_____	_____

**Complete each sentence with a word from above.
Write the word on the line.**

1. Some people think bats are blind, but that is _____.

2. Bats see quite well and can catch insects in _____.

3. You cannot _____ your nose to the nose of an elephant.

4. An elephant's nose is a _____ of a water hose and a sniffer.

5. Bob and Carlos are both _____ of the school newspaper.

6. Carlos knows he must write clearly so that he is not _____.

7. Bob looks in the encyclopedia to _____ facts about animals.

8. Sometimes Bob and Carlos _____ on what should go on the front page.

Have your child choose a word from the list above and use it in a sentence.

Add the prefixes in dark print to each word in the row to make new words.

> **RULE** Remember, a prefix changes the meaning of a word.
>
> **im** and **in** mean "not" or "into"
>   **im**possible = not possible
>   **in**active = not active
>
> **em** and **en** mean "in," "to cause to be," or "to make"
>   **em**power = to make powerful
>   **en**danger = to cause to be in danger

1. **im**   press _____   possible _____

2. **in**   habit _____   credible _____

3. **em**   brace _____   body _____

4. **en**   able _____   joy _____

Complete each sentence with a word from above. Write the word on the line.

Do you know about these cold weather animals?

5. The Weddell seal lives in the Antarctic. Warm fur and thick layers

   of fat _____ this animal to keep warm.

6. Monkeys called macaques _____ the mountains of northern Japan.

7. To keep warm, macaques _____ long, hot baths in the volcanic springs nearby.

8. A team of twelve husky dogs can pull a sled that weighs

   1,000 pounds. Now, that's _____!

9. Once a polar bear rang a bell at the front door of a school in Russia.

   I would have thought it was _____ for a bear to do that!

10. Would it _____ you if I told you that the largest polar mammal is the polar bear?

Name _____

Circle the word that completes each sentence. Write the word on the line.

Now, That's Incredible!

1. Camels can drink 25 gallons of water at a time. That is an

   _____ amount of water!

   improve
   incredible
   inhabit

2. Desert wallabies and kangaroos lick their bodies when they are hot.

   This _____ them to stay cool.

   embeds
   encloses
   enables

3. Small desert animals _____ themselves in underground burrows to keep cool during the day.

   encourage
   enclose
   embank

4. The Mojave desert squirrel sleeps in an underground burrow during

   times of drought. When the weather _____, it comes out.

   impossible
   improves
   embitter

5. When it is very hot, I like to stay _____ to keep cool.

   encourage
   inhabit
   indoors

6. About 5,000 years ago, animals such as giraffes and lions

   _____ what is now the Sahara desert.

   impatient
   inhabited
   embedded

7. This fact will _____ you: The addax, an antelope, never drinks. It gets all its water from plants.

   impress
   import
   enjoy

8. Desert mammals _____ drinking the water they find inside the giant saguaro cactus. This plant can store nine tons of water.

   encourage
   enjoy
   enable

AT HOME Challenge your child to use one word not circled to make up a sentence about an incredible animal fact.

Use the base words, suffixes, and prefixes below to make new words.

1. thought + ful + ness _____

2. re + locate + ion _____

3. dis + agree + ment _____

4. un + comfort + able _____

5. non + pay + ment _____

6. re + heat + able _____

7. ex + change + able _____

8. non + re + fund + able _____

9. in + excuse + able _____

10. un + rely + able _____

11. thought + ful + ly _____

12. co + operate + ion _____

Answer each question with one of the words you wrote above.

13. What word describes something you are able to exchange? _____

14. What word describes something that is without an excuse? _____

15. What word describes something you can't count upon? _____

16. What do you call a cold supper of leftovers? _____

17. What word describes something that can't be refunded? _____

18. What word describes clothing that is itchy, hot, or scratchy? _____

Name _____

Circle the word that completes each sentence.
Write the word on the line.

1. A gorilla named Koko has shown the _____ of sign language in communication with gorillas.

   usefulness
   usually
   unexpectedly

2. Koko _____ uses sign language to describe her kitten as fat, soft, and good.

   thoughtlessness
   thoughtfully
   unthoughtful

3. In 1971, a group of judges _____ awarded an orangutan at the Topeka Zoo the first prize in an art contest.

   unwittingly
   cheerlessly
   thoughtfulness

4. In Australia, a monkey named Johnnie sat _____ in the driver's seat of a tractor and learned how to drive.

   comfortably
   precaution
   unbelievable

5. Old newspapers, cans, boxes, and many other worn-out items

   are _____.

   recyclable
   reheatable
   nonrefundable

6. _____ is the best way to save many of the world's natural resources.

   Department
   Regardless
   Conservation

7. We took many _____ before we rode our bicycles on the street.

   semiprecious
   thoughtfulness
   precautions

8. All of my library books are _____.

   refundable
   copayment
   renewable

9. I was surprised when my mother came home _____.

   unexpectedly
   uncomfortably
   unreliably

10. When I tossed away a perfectly good paper plate, I was guilty

    of _____.

    conservation
    wastefulness
    disagreement

AT HOME

Have your child circle each prefix and underline each suffix in the word choices above.

© Steck-Vaughn Company

Read the passage. Then use complete sentences to answer each question below.

Insects Watch Out for . . .

Deadly Traps!

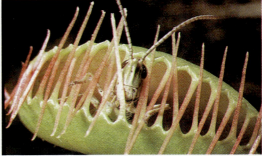
Venus flytap

You might expect a frog to eat insects, but what about plants that eat insects? Some plants are carnivorous, too. In other words, they trap and eat insects. About five hundred of these plants exist around the world. They usually inhabit areas where the soil is boggy. The insects enrich their diet and give them what the soil cannot.

A Venus flytrap is a carnivorous plant. When an insect contacts the hairs on this plant, CRUNCH! Quite unexpectedly, the leaves snap shut and entrap the insect.

Scientists discovered that the butterwort plant produces sticky, greasy droplets that attract and trap insects. A leaf curls around and encloses the insect. Special proteins, called enzymes, dissolve the insect's body. Then the plant can absorb the insect's nutrients.

Sundew

It is impossible for an insect to escape from a pitcher plant. A sweet smell attracts the insect, who descends inside the long, slippery sides of the plant's pitcher. Midway down the pitcher, the plant has hairs that point downward. They prevent the insect from climbing back up. Enzymes dissolve the insect's body, and the plant drinks its fertilizer.

Sundews are carnivorous plants you can find at local plant nurseries. Their purpose is unmistakably clear: Tiny tentacles on their leaves attract victims and then strangle them. Sundews are easy to grow. They are excellent plants for raising indoors or outdoors.

1. Why do some plants need to eat insects?

_____

2. What do the leaves of a Venus flytrap do to an insect?

_____

3. How does the butterwort attract insects?

_____

4. How does the pitcher plant keep insects from escaping?

_____

5. Where can you buy sundews?

_____

Name _____

What unusual plant or animal do you know about? Describe what you know about this unusual plant or animal in a paragraph. The words in the box may help you.

PHONICS and WRITING

compare	enjoy	explore	incredible	inhabit
midway	mistake	nonsense	prehistoric	react
recently	submarine	tricolor	unbelievable	unexpected

Writing Tip After you have reread your revised draft, ask a classmate to read it. Your classmate can comment on your ideas and help you decide whether your draft needs more revision.

AT HOME

Ask your child to read the paragraph to you.

Read each sentence. Underline the word that contains the root pos or pel. Then circle the meaning of the underlined word.

1. No one knows why the eyes of a stalk-eyed fly are positioned so far away from each other.

   a. placed   **b.** push away

2. If you break off the bark of a log, you will expose many insects.

   a. bring to a place to be seen   **b.** take away from a place

3. I feel compelled to learn as much as I can about insects.

   a. pushed away   **b.** driven or forced

4. I like insects, so the insect repellent I use is not made of poisons.

   a. place that attracts insects   **b.** solution that drives away insects

Stalk-eyed fly

5. My bed is on the opposite side of the room from my brother's bed.

   a. on the other side   **b.** on the same side

6. Hank will dispose of the trash outside.

   a. put in a safe place   **b.** get rid of

7. Even though it was only April, Alicia was positive that she saw a firefly in her backyard.

   a. takes the position of belief   **b.** weighs the proof

Assassin fly

8. The motor propels the boat through the water.

   a. places   **b.** pushes

Name _____

**Circle the word that completes the sentence.
Write the word on the line.**

Dr. Jane Goodall

1. Jane Goodall had the ———————— to observe chimpanzees in the wild.

   opportunity
   objection

2. The chimpanzees did not ———————— to her presence in their habitat.

   object
   import

3. Ms. Goodall made an ———————— discovery about the chimpanzees.

   injection
   important

4. She ———————— that chimpanzees use tools to gather their food.

   rejection
   reported

5. Our teacher set up a ———————— to show us a movie about chimpanzees.

   projector
   ejected

6. The only ———————— in the thick jungle is by foot.

   objective
   transportation

7. The United States ———————— much of its oil from the Mideast.

   imports
   injects

8. The United States ———————— cars and trucks to many countries.

   subjects
   exports

9. When I shop for school clothes, I ———————— anything yellow.

   reject
   deport

10. Don't fight or you might be ———————— from the basketball game.

    projected
    ejected

AT HOME

Ask your child to choose one of the words from this lesson and use it in a sentence.

Read each word in the box and circle the root. Then write the word on the line beside its definition.

1. to take away one's attention _____

2. to present someone _____

3. person who leads _____

4. to take away _____

5. an agreement between two people _____

6. draw attention to _____

7. a machine used for pulling _____

8. to pull out _____

attract
conductor
contract
distract
extract
introduce
subtract
tractor

Complete each sentence with a word from above.

9. If you _____ all the water from Earth's oceans, you will have 48 million tons of salt left!

10. Amazing facts like that _____ me to science.

11. Mike made a _____ with his parents to earn an allowance for doing his chores.

12. My noisy little brothers _____ me from my homework.

13. My aunt is the _____ of an orchestra.

14. I will _____ my parents to Mr. Rojas.

Name _____

Circle the root in each word below. Then write the letter of each definition in front of the correct word.

> **RULE** Remember, roots are word parts that have meaning but cannot stand alone.
>
> **spec** and **spect** mean "examine," "look," or "see"
>   **spec**ulator = one who looks for profits
>   **spect**ator = one who watches
> **scribe** means "write"
>   in**scribe** = to write on or in

_____ 1. spectator   **a.** one who watches

_____ 2. special   **b.** to have regard for

_____ 3. inspect   **c.** tells about, especially about how something looks

_____ 4. subscribe   **d.** to look over carefully

_____ 5. inscribe   **e.** something that may happen in the future

_____ 6. prospect   **f.** examples

_____ 7. specimens   **g.** to write on

_____ 8. describes   **h.** unusual, exceptional

_____ 9. spectrum   **i.** to agree to buy or order

_____ 10. respect   **j.** a band of colors; the rainbow

Complete each sentence with a word from above.

11. I _____ to a magazine that tells unusual facts about nature.

12. One article _____ how owls and cats can see so well at night.

13. Nighttime animals have a _____ layer in the back of their eyes that acts like a mirror.

14. To the _____, this layer, called tapetum, seems to make the animal's eyes shine in the dark.

15. Dogs cannot see a full _____ of colors.

16. The editors _____ the magazine for errors.

17. Scientists study fossil _____ to make sense of history.

18. Have you considered the _____ of a career in science?

In each of these sentences, the word **mystery** stands for one of the words in the box. Write the correct word on the line.

bicycle	contest	decode	disappeared	discount	exchange
impact	introduce	midsummer	misprint	nonstop	preheat
prehistoric	reread	semicircle	spectators	subtract	tripod

1. Scientists think they know why dinosaurs mystery from Earth.

2. Many mystery animals died off about 65 million years ago.

3. Scientists have worked to mystery clues about what happened.

4. They think that a meteor or a comet hit Earth, and the mystery killed the animals.

5. The mystery were happy to see that their team won.

6. Will you mystery me to your friend?

7. I can add better than I can mystery.

8. I want to ride my mystery to school.

9. We put the camera on a mystery.

10. I liked that book so much that I want to mystery it.

11. Can we mystery the oven before we bake the cake?

12. I have to mystery this sweater because it doesn't fit.

13. I got a mystery price on my new coat.

14. This plane flies mystery to New York City.

15. The newspaper corrected its mystery the next day.

16. We go swimming in mystery.

17. A mystery is half a circle.

18. I won the spelling mystery.

1. _____   2. _____   3. _____

4. _____   5. _____   6. _____

7. _____   8. _____   9. _____

10. _____   11. _____   12. _____

13. _____   14. _____   15. _____

16. _____   17. _____   18. _____

Name _____

Long ago as sailors sailed vast oceans, they heard strange songs coming from the deep waters. They thought these sounds came from mermaids, but scientists have found out their real source.

1	2	3	4	5	6	7	8	9	10	11	12	13	14	15	16	17	18	19	20	21	22
a	b	c	e	f	g	h	i	k	l	m	n	o	p	r	s	t	u	v	w	x	y

1. before history
14 15 4 7 8 16 17 13 15 8 3

2. full of play
14 10 1 22 5 18 10

3. something that amuses
1 11 18 16 4 11 4 12 17

4. an error in printing
11 8 16 14 15 8 12 17

5. state of being black
2 10 1 3 9 12 4 16 16

6. every half year
16 4 11 8 1 12 12 18 1 10

7. to save
3 13 12 16 4 15 19 4

8. to go aboard a ship
4 11 2 1 15 9

9. to make white
20 7 8 17 4 12

10. to trade for another
4 21 3 7 1 12 6 4

11. to draw attention to
1 17 17 15 1 3 17

12. cannot be counted
3 13 18 12 17 10 4 16 16

13. opposite of patient
8 11 14 1 17 8 4 12 17

14. to close around something
4 12 3 10 13 16 4

It was really __ __ __ __ __ __ __ __   __ __ __ __ __ .

AT HOME

© Steck-Vaughn Company

Read the passage. Then use complete sentences to answer each question below.

A Telling Trail

Have you ever dropped a sandwich at a picnic and wondered how ants found your food only minutes later? Have you ever thought about why ants all march in the same straight line, some going toward the food, while others carry the food back in the opposite direction? If you inspect ants closely, you will find the answers!

Ants live in huge nests called colonies in the ground or in trees. Some ants in the colony have the important job of looking for food. These ants are called scouts.

When a scout finds a portable juicy tidbit, such as your sandwich, it reports back to the colony. The ant's body produces a special chemical. As it returns to the nest, the scout expels this chemical from the rear of its body. When the scout reaches the other ants, they are attracted to the smell of the trail the scout left for them. They follow the trail back to the food.

Leafcutter ant

Ants collect as much of the food as they can carry and transport it back to the nest. As they walk back, they expel more of the chemical so other ants can find the source of food. As more ants transport the food back to the nest, the supply of food is reduced until it is totally gone. When the food disappears, the returning ants no longer leave a scented trail. Soon the scouts will search for another source of food.

1. What is the scout's job?

   _____

2. How does the scout lead the other ants to the food?

   _____

3. Why do the other ants follow the trail?

   _____

4. What do the other ants do when they find the food?

   _____

5. What happens when the food is all gone?

   _____

Name _____

Do you ever wonder why wolves howl or how birds know when and where to migrate? Think of a question about nature. Research the answer in the library. Then write a paragraph that explains the answer. The words in the box may help you.

PHONICS and WRITING

attract	conduct
describe	important
inspect	introduce
opportunity	position
produce	repel
report	specific
spectacular	spectrum
subject	

I Wonder Why. . .

_____

_____

_____

Writing Tip To proofread thoroughly, read your paragraph through several times. Read through to check grammar and punctuation and again to check spelling.

_____

_____

_____

_____

_____

_____

_____

© Steck-Vaughn Company

AT HOME Have your child read the paragraph to you.

Circle the word that completes each sentence. Write the word on the line.

1. The _____ of the microscope unlocked many mysteries of science.

discovers
discovery
uncovering

2. The _____ of the telescope helped astronomers.

invention
prevention
injection

3. The _____ of the orchestra bowed to the audience.

conserve
inspector
conductor

4. Mozart was a famous _____ of music.

composition
composer
composed

5. We sat around the teacher in a _____.

semiannual
semitropical
semicircle

6. I _____ paper and glass to conserve energy.

react
recycle
refundable

7. Some natural resources, such as oil, cannot be _____.

previewed
renewed
derailed

8. A crying baby caused a _____ during the play.

assistance
disagreeable
disturbance

9. That red, yellow, and black snake is probably _____.

poisonous
cleverness
pointless

10. A _____ is a three-wheeled vehicle.

tripod
bicycle
tricycle

Name _____

Unit 5 CHECK-UP

Fill in the circle next to the word that completes the sentence.

1. I want to be a _____ who studies the wonders of nature.
   ○ scientific ○ scientist
   ○ senseless ○ sciences

2. _____ was a dinosaur with three horns.
   ○ Tristate ○ Tyrannosaurus
   ○ Tricycle ○ Triceratops

3. It is fun to watch the _____ of geese in the fall.
   ○ migration ○ mysterious
   ○ masterful ○ midnight

4. Each summer, my family takes a trip to an _____ park.
   ○ amazement ○ adornment
   ○ amusement ○ addition

5. We pretend to travel underwater on the _____ ride.
   ○ submerge ○ subnormal
   ○ semifinal ○ submarine

6. Many wild animals _____ big cities.
   ○ indoors ○ incredible
   ○ inhabit ○ inactive

7. In my report, I _____ coyotes and wolves.
   ○ conspired ○ compared
   ○ compacted ○ cooperated

8. I had fun _____ the animals' habitats and habits.
   ○ describing ○ subscribing
   ○ depressing ○ exclaiming

9. The colors of the rainbow are called the _____.
   ○ spectacles ○ spectators
   ○ spectrum ○ specialist

10. I won't need _____ with my homework assignment.
    ○ assistance ○ importance
    ○ insurance ○ resistance

Dictionary

A Dictionary's where you can look things up
To see if they're really there:
To see if what you breathe is AIR,
If what you sit on is a CHAIR,
If what you comb is curly HAIR,
If what you drink from is a CUP.
A Dictionary's where you can look things up
To see if they're really there.

William Jay Smith

Think About It

Does the poet know the meaning of the words in the poem?
How can you tell? What other resources can you use
to find answers to questions?

Dear Family of _____,

Your child will be learning about dictionary skills, synonyms, antonyms, and homonyms. Your child will be using these skills to read about the theme of Let's Find Out. Here are some activities you can do together.

- With your child, read the back of a cereal box or an advertisement from a magazine. Choose some words to say aloud. See how quickly your child can find each word in the dictionary.
- Offer your child some challenges using a dictionary. For example:

  1. How many synonyms can you find for *talk*? For *run*? For *happy*?
  2. How many antonyms can you find for *simple*? For *hot*? For *cruel*?
  3. Give another spelling and definition for *fair*. For *piece*.
  4. Find one word that falls between *magnet* and *mail* in the dictionary.
  5. What is the preferred pronunciation of the word *envelope*?

LIBRARY LINK

You might like to visit the library and find the book *Maps and Globes* by Jack Knowlton. Read it with your child.

- Make a book by stapling together a few sheets of paper. Help your child make a silly definition dictionary. For example, your child might write the following:

  cool cat 1. a cat with sunglasses <example: Cleocatra > **2.** a cat sitting in front of a fan

Estimada familia de _____,

Su niño o niña aprenderá destrezas para el uso del diccionario, sinónimos, antónimos y homónimos. Él o ella usará estos conocimientos en su lectura sobre Vamos a averiguar. Algunas actividades que usted y su niño o niña pueden hacer en inglés aparecen a continuación.

- Juntos lean el aviso en el reverso de una caja de cereal o un aviso de una revista. Elijan algunas palabras para decirlas en voz alta. Luego, vea cuánto se demora su niño o niña en encontrar cada palabra en el diccionario.
- Ofrezca a su niño o niña algunos retos en el uso del diccionario. Por ejemplo:

  1. ¿Cuántos sinónimos puede encontrar para *talk*? Para *run*? Para *happy*?
  2. ¿Cuántos antónimos puede encontrar para *simple*? Para *hot*? Para *cruel*?
  3. Encuentre otra manera de escribir y definir la palabra *fair*. También *piece*.
  4. Encuentre una palabra que aparezca entre *magnet* y *mail* en el diccionario.
  5. ¿Cuál es la pronunciación de preferencia de la palabra *envelope*?

- Construyan un libro sujetando con grapas algunas hojas de papel. Ayude a su niño o niña a escribir un diccionario de definiciones divertidas. Por ejemplo, pudiera escribir lo siguiente:

  cool cat 1. a cat with sunglasses <example: Cleocatra > **2.** a cat sitting in front of a fan

Each word in the list has a synonym in the box. Write the synonym on the line. Then read the letters in the shaded boxes to answer the question below.

1. shy ___ ___ ___ ___

2. perfect ___ ___ ___ ___

3. shore ___ ___ ___ ___

4. drift ___ ___ ___ ___

5. tasty ___ ___ ___ ___ ___

6. noisy ___ ___ ___

7. quiet ___ ___ ___ ___

8. break ___ ___ ___ ___

9. difficult ___ ___ ___

10. purchase ___ ___

11. yell ___ ___ ___ ___

12. wealthy ___ ___ ___

13. jump ___ ___ ___

14. certain ___ ___ ___

15. old ___ ___ ___ ___ ___

16. need ___ ___ ___ ___ ___

17. lawn ___ ___ ___

18. noise ___ ___ ___ ___

19. damp ___ ___ ___ ___

ancient	require
beach	rich
buy	shout
delicious	silent
float	smash
hard	sound
ideal	sure
leap	timid
loud	yard
moist	

Where can you find a synonym?

——————————————— or ———————————————

Name _____

Unscramble the letters to find a synonym for each word. Write the word on the line.

1. award   **zerip**   _____

2. sick   **lil**   _____

3. remain   **yats**   _____

4. correct   **ghirt**   _____

5. tale   **tyors**   _____

6. assists   **elshp**   _____

7. discover   **arlen**   _____

8. journey   **prit**   _____

Read each sentence below. Each underlined word has a synonym in the list above. Write the synonym on the line.

9. Rosa wanted to <u>discover</u> more about young hospital patients. _____

10. She planned to write a <u>tale</u> about it for her school newspaper. _____

11. First, she read books about hospitals and <u>sick</u> children. _____

12. Then she took a <u>journey</u> to a children's hospital. _____

13. She asked the children how long they had to <u>remain</u> in the hospital. _____

14. She asked the doctors about the <u>correct</u> treatments for patients. _____

15. Rosa's writing won an <u>award</u> from a community group. _____

16. Rosa now <u>assists</u> children at the hospital as a volunteer. _____

AT HOME

Have your child give examples of other synonyms that are not listed on this page.

Find antonyms in the puzzle for the words in the list. Circle the words and write them on the lines. Words in the puzzle can go down or across.

1. subtract _____

2. over _____

3. difficult _____

4. close _____

5. first _____

6. push _____

7. before _____

8. quiet _____

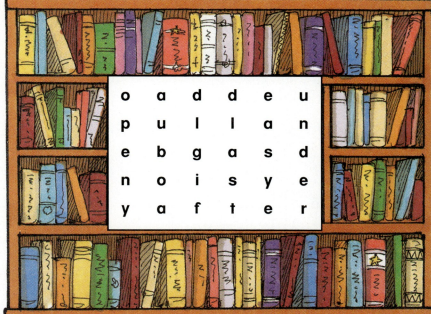

o	a	d	d	e	u
p	u	l	l	a	n
e	b	g	a	s	d
n	o	i	s	y	e
y	a	f	t	e	r

Change the meaning of each sentence by choosing an antonym in the box to replace the underlined word. Write the antonym on the line.

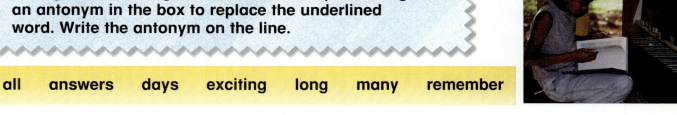

all	answers	days	exciting	long	many	remember

9. We went to the library two <u>nights</u> ago. _____

10. It is a <u>short</u> walk from our house to the branch library. _____

11. My brother and I had <u>few</u> questions about bats. _____

12. We found <u>none</u> of the answers to our questions. _____

13. The <u>questions</u> were interesting. _____

14. We want to <u>forget</u> the facts we learned. _____

15. A library can be a very <u>dull</u> place. _____

Name _____

Find two words in the box that are antonyms for each word in the list below. Write the antonyms on the lines.

| close | falsehood | fast | happy | joyful | lie |
| lose | misplace | puny | quick | shut | weak |

1. slow _____ _____

2. sad _____ _____

3. find _____ _____

4. truth _____ _____

5. open _____ _____

6. strong _____ _____

Circle the word that completes each sentence. Write the word on the line.

7. Dad _____ a new dictionary for our family to use.   sold   bought

8. We were pleased and _____ when we saw it.   smiled   frowned

9. Dad likes to find words he has never seen _____.   before   after

10. We use the dictionary to _____ a game.   work   play

11. Someone finds a really _____ word that no one knows.   strange   familiar

12. We _____ a new meaning for the word.   destroy   create

13. Then we read the definition and hope we were _____.   correct   wrong

14. Sometimes we laugh and the game gets a bit _____.   wild   tame

15. Then Mom asks us to try to calm _____.   up   down

AT HOME

Choose several words from above. Ask your child to name an antonym for each word.

RULE Homonyms are words that sound the same but have different spellings and meanings.

pair—pear   hear—here

1. Claire found a fossil as she sifted through dirt as fine as _____.   flower

2. It looked like a strange type of _____.   flour

3. The fossil was a _____ gray color.   pail

4. She lifted it carefully out of the dirt and put it in her _____.   pale

5. She looked in an encyclopedia _____ information about it.   for

6. Claire found _____ photos of fossils like the one she found.   four

7. The fossil was once a _____ creature called a crinoid.   see

8. We _____ modern crinoids, such as starfish, in tide pools.   sea

9. Most crinoids have five arms, but Claire's fossil had _____.   ate

10. It _____ by using its arms to sweep food into its mouth.   eight

11. Claire _____ several books to learn more about crinoids.   red

12. Her favorite book on fossils had a bright _____ cover.   read

13. Claire often stops _____ the place where she found the fossil.   by

14. She thinks it's more fun to find fossils than to _____ them.   buy

Name _____

1. When I have a question, I (know, no) what to do. _____

2. To find the answer, I can ask the (write, right) person. _____

3. I can look in a book and (read, reed) to find the answer. _____

4. I can also visit different (sites, sights) on the Internet. _____

5. I wanted to (rays, raise) a garden to attract butterflies. _____

6. I had (scene, seen) one, but I wasn't sure how to get started. _____

7. No one I (new, knew) could tell me how to begin. _____

8. I asked Mom if I was (allowed, aloud) to use her computer. _____

9. She said she (wood, would) not mind at all. _____

10. So, I logged on and surfed the Web for about an (hour, our). _____

11. (Won, One) home page had a lot of information. _____

12. It told the best plants for the (weather, whether) in my area. _____

13. It listed everything I need to (billed, build) a butterfly garden. _____

14. Now I have a (grate, great) plan for my garden. _____

15. Soon, a butterfly may be my (guest, guessed)! _____

AT HOME

Ask your child to make up sentences with some of the homonyms above.

Write the words in each list in alphabetical order. Then number the lists from one to six to show the overall alphabetical order.

1

order of list ____

glisten   _____

gladly   _____

grateful   _____

glow   _____

gainfully   _____

2

order of list ____

center   _____

comb   _____

chart   _____

cube   _____

castle   _____

3

order of list ____

shallow   _____

share   _____

shuttle   _____

shark   _____

shelter   _____

4

order of list ____

trim   _____

tried   _____

trial   _____

triple   _____

trickle   _____

5

order of list ____

label   _____

lane   _____

lace   _____

lamb   _____

lame   _____

6

order of list ____

brain   _____

breathless   _____

brilliant   _____

bravery   _____

breeze   _____

Name _____

Write the names of these countries in alphabetical order.

Portugal	Norway	Oman	Paraguay	Romania
Puerto Rico	Peru	Pakistan	Nicaragua	Niger
Panama	Nigeria	Philippines	New Zealand	Poland

1. _____
2. _____
3. _____
4. _____
5. _____
6. _____
7. _____
8. _____
9. _____
10. _____
11. _____
12. _____
13. _____
14. _____
15. _____

Write each list of oceans and seas in alphabetical order.

16. _____
17. _____
18. _____
19. _____
20. _____

Pacific
Arctic
Indian
North Atlantic
South Atlantic

21. _____
22. _____
23. _____
24. _____
25. _____

Caribbean
Bering
Labrador
Arabian
Philippine

Mexico
Belize
Guatemala
Honduras
El Salvador
Nicaragua
Costa Rica
Panama
Atlantic Ocean
Caribbean Sea
Pacific Ocean

© Steck-Vaughn Company

AT HOME

Have your child write five street names or places in alphabetical order.

Read each pair of guide words below. Place an **X** on any words that would not appear on the same dictionary page as these guide words. Then write the remaining three words in alphabetical order.

1   clasp—clay

claw   _____

clear   _____

clause   _____

classroom

2   place—post

power   _____

pocket   _____

plum   _____

plane

3   camera—chime

center   _____

cheer   _____

camper   _____

choice

4   huge—humor

human   _____

hull   _____

hue   _____

humid

5   tub—turtle

tuna   _____

tusk   _____

turn   _____

tuba

6   mitt—mock

mixture   _____

mist   _____

moan   _____

mobile

Read each pair of guide words below. Circle the words that would be on the dictionary page with these guide words. Then number the circled words in each column to put them in alphabetical order.

7   brace—bubble

break   ___

braid   ___

bucket   ___

bright   ___

8   neither—net

new   ___

nervous   ___

nestle   ___

nephew   ___

9   vital—volleyball

vivid   ___

vitamin   ___

vocabulary   ___

visitor   ___

Name _____